The Future of Work

The Future of Work

Practical People Strategies for Business Leaders

Authors:

Michelle Bailey

Alasdair Graham

Jan P. de Jonge

Marjory Mair

Heather Mills

Samantha Pennell

Siân Perham

Marc Reid

Peter Thomson

Adrian Wheatley

Table of Contents

Foreword - 'A Book in a Day'

The genesis of this book is somewhat unusual. It came about after I had published an eBook and paperback using the Amazon KDP system (Kindle Direct Publishing) and found it far easier than I had ever imagined. Having previously published a book through the more conventional process of using a publisher, I was impressed with how simple the Amazon process was – plus the benefit that no upfront investment was needed. I shared my experience with my fellow consultant, Michelle Bailey, and it must have inspired her as a month later she had published her own book.

I help Michelle run the local CIPD Special Interest Group (SIG) for HR Consultants and we are always looking for topics that will interest our members. So we came up with the idea of running a session to share our publishing experiences and encourage our fellow consultants to take the leap into writing and publishing. Then I had a random idea – 'show and tell' is all very well but it is far more interesting to actually 'do'. Why not turn the session into a workshop where we show people how to create a book by actually producing and publishing a real book during the workshop? It seemed somewhat crazy but Michelle was up for it and 'A book in a day' was born.

The contributors to this book are all members of the Thames Valley CIPD and attended our 'A book in a day' workshop on 7 June, 2019. All are expert HR professionals, with specific areas of interest, and range from writing 'newbies' through to experienced, published authors. The majority of the participants had not written before and this book provides them the opportunity to be published without having to write a whole book – and who knows, perhaps it will give them the courage to write a book of their own.

We selected the subject of 'The future of work' as it is a highly topical and broad enough topic for all of us to write an informed piece from some angle or other. We were keen that the book should be a valuable tool for business leaders rather than an academic think piece. Our focus therefore is on practical ideas and strategies that give the reader a toolbox they can pick from and apply effectively in the workplace.

Running the workshop and producing this book has been a fantastic effort from all those involved. It has proved that delivering something of value in a condensed timeframe is absolutely possible though we can't promise to have found every error. To make it all happen has meant a lot of hard work on the day but also significant preparation beforehand. I would like to thank all those involved in the creation of this book, in particular Michelle, who has picked up my hare-brained scheme and driven it to become a reality. We are also indebted to our writing and editing expert **Robert Bullard**, who brought his professional expertise to the project, leading the training element of the workshop and guiding Michelle and I in setting it up. Robert has been an invaluable support and we are very grateful to him (see his biog on the following page).

We have decided to donate all proceeds from the sale of this book to two very worthy charities, DementiaUK and Autistica.

We hope you enjoy the book and find it useful in your leadership role. Hopefully too we might have inspired you to at least think about writing and publishing something yourself – it really is more straightforward than you imagine!

Marc Reid

Robert Bullard lives in Oxford, and is an experienced copywriter, trainer in writing skills, book writing coach, and copy-editor/proofreader. To clients, Robert brings the skills and expertise of a professional writer (he wrote features for *The Guardian* and *The Daily Telegraph* for six years) and a quick understanding of all kinds of businesses (he has worked in private consultancy, in senior positions in local government, and as a manager/volunteer in third sector organisations). In 2015, Robert authored and self-published *Business Writing Tips: For Easy and Effective Results.*

For more details: perfecttext.org

Introduction

Try a Google search on 'the future of work' and you'll be inundated with insight pieces from strategic consulting firms, forecast data from international economic organisations and media headline grabbers. *"Automation could replace 1.5 million jobs, says ONS"* was a top story on the BBC News website on 25 March 2019. So there is evidently interest and perhaps even fear about what lies ahead for work in the future. As a group of experienced HR professionals it perhaps affects and inspires us as a subject more than most. That's why we decided to apply our own specialist skills and knowledge to examine this topic and approach it from a pragmatic and practical perspective. We give our views on the future of work but more importantly we provide guidance, tools and resources which will enable business leaders to be successful in the new 'world of work'.

What will this world look like? Clearly it will be different from today as we are experiencing great change in what work we do, how we do it and where it is. This change is a reflection of a rapidly evolving society. It is said we are living a in VUCA world, a term derived from the American military which is intended to highlight the key elements of change that are taking place:

- **V**olatility – the change is constant and rapid, big and small, and unpredictable in timing or outcome.
- **U**ncertainty – events are giving unexpected outcomes, and forecasting or predicting with any accuracy is becoming increasingly difficult.
- **C**omplexity – issues are increasingly complex with multiple layers and are difficult to understand with the risk of being overwhelmed.

- **A**mbiguity – things are rarely clear or 'black and white' and a single solution is no longer sufficient. A more nuanced and personalised response is needed.

Recent world events give ample evidence of the VUCA world – the financial crisis, the election of Donald Trump and the Brexit referendum are all good examples of how we have experienced and continue to experience volatile, uncertain, complex and ambiguous change.

How do we in the people profession see the future for the world of work set against this context of societal change? Peter Cheese, the Chief Executive Officer of our professional body, the Chartered Institute of Personnel and Development (CIPD), is clear where the future lies:

> *"We need to make sure that the future of work is human, that we are designing workplaces that make the best of people and not just the best of clever technology. Work forms such a major part of our lives and human society, it should contribute to our wellbeing, our growth and our sense of purpose."*[1]

Peter places the human at the core. If that is the case how do we respond to the substantial change that is occurring? We need first to understand specifically <u>what</u> is changing, and we have picked out three major trends which directly impact how we will work in the future:

- Technology
- Globalisation / populism
- Changing workforce

---

[1] 'Robots Don't Kill Jobs, People Do' – CIPD Blog, 28 April, 2016

Technology

The effect of technology is unmistakeable. Workplaces and our way of working have been transformed by computers, the internet and social media. But the biggest threat, or opportunity, depending on your perspective, is the growth of Artificial Intelligence. This has the power to transform work by replacing humans with robots. It is already happening. Has anyone not experienced 'AI rage' when the automatic checkout complains of an 'unexpected item in the bagging area'? The BBC headline mentioned above shows that it is not just supermarket checkout assistants who are being replaced. The ONS report[2] refers to other routine type roles that have a high risk of replacement, such as waiters and shelf fillers. Yet professional jobs are also at threat, typically those where the role revolves around processing and analysing data, such as paralegals and accountants.

How do we respond to this risk? The answer is partly in new jobs which will replace the old jobs. Jobs, which may not exist today but will be needed in the future. Yesterday's horse and cart driver, is today's lorry driver and perhaps tomorrow's driverless fleet manager. However it is not only the type of jobs which will change but the skills we require in the future will also need to change. Naturally we will need to gain the technical skills to survive in the future - digital expertise for instance will become essential rather than desirable. But to be employable in the future employees will need people skills. These are the abilities that AI will struggle to replicate and replace. Communication, emotional intelligence and collaboration will be high up on the recruiters agenda for tomorrow's workforce.

---

[2] BBC News website – 25 March, 2019

Globalisation / Populism

Technology has been an amazing facilitator of globalisation – the ability to communicate and trade quickly and efficiently without geographical constraints. It has enabled for example large organisations to outsource their telephone customer service departments to low-cost countries like India. Yet, more recently we have seen a reaction against globalisation. Populism and nationalism have been on the rise indicating a shift back towards a desire for greater control, and an uncomfortable feeling of being part of a too large machine and wanting more power to determine how we work.

This change is reflected in a number of areas, not least the rise of the gig economy as people utilise the opportunity to take work as and when they want it. Technology enables remote working and close monitoring so the need to meet in an office is less important. The amount and variety of flexible working has also grown rapidly in recent years as people don't want a 'one size fits all' type of approach and want to make work work for them. This creates challenges for the managers of tomorrow. How can you manage a workforce which may never meet one another? Again it comes back to the people skills of the manager to communicate effectively, facilitate collaboration and engage the team.

Changing workforce

The workforce of the future will be the Millennials and Generation Zs who have a different outlook and drivers than previous generations. Set against this we have an ageing population and people will be working longer. We will have therefore multigenerational workforces which in itself will be a challenge for managers.

Digital skills won't be an issue for the Generation Z's. They are the so-called 'digital natives' who have grown up with technology and have not known a world without it. More relevant will be skills which have been important in the past but are even more essential in the future such as critical thinking. We have entered what has been described as a 'post truth' world where the line between what is fact and fiction has been blurred, captured in the phraseology used by President Trump Press Secretary Sean Spicer when he referred to 'alternative facts'. To thrive in the workplace of tomorrow employees will need to be able to apply objective analysis, exercise critical judgement and communicate quality output effectively – these are the skills which will be in high demand with employers.

How can this book help business leaders?

These three trends are not the only challenges facing the business leaders of tomorrow. One of the VUCA elements is complexity and the evidence of this is that these major themes will need to be tackled alongside ongoing issues such as the mental health of the workforce, achieving gender pay equality, inclusion and diversity. Leaders must recognise that the 'future of work is human' and develop their own people skills sufficiently if they are to achieve success. This book is our contribution to those leaders. It helps them understand what skills they need and offers tools to support them.

Each chapter of this book has a different author. They are all experienced HR professionals and collectively they contribute a wealth of expertise to tackle the major challenge faced by tomorrow's business leaders. We have focused in particular on the broad areas of:

- Developing people – understanding the psychology of our employees, and how to engage them through awareness of what drives them and how to generate improved performance.
- Communication – how communication can be improved, and in particular the importance of feedback.

- Collaboration – how teams can work together more effectively, and understanding how to avoid potential destructive conflict.

We hope you find this book a helpful resource, providing you with valuable practical people strategies that will help ensure that the 'future of work is human'.

Michelle Bailey and Marc Reid

Staying human is the future of work

By Michelle Bailey

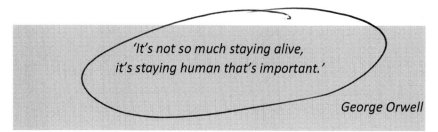

*'It's not so much staying alive,
it's staying human that's important.'*

George Orwell

Big data, fast data, artificial intelligence and the internet of things are among some of the technologies improving the performance of many businesses - doing tasks faster, better and with fewer errors than any person could.

Technology is one of the five trends Jacob Morgan[3] identifies as shaping the future of work and driving change. Not only is it expected to boost the productivity of organisations, local communities and the wider economy, it will also address some of the challenges of an ageing and shrinking working population.

There is some anxiety that technology will take away jobs. In reality there is and will continue to be a lot of things about 'being human' that cannot be automated.

---

[3] Jacob Morgan: *The Future of Work: Attract New Talent, Build Better Leaders, and Create a Competitive Organization*

Big Data

...extremely large data sets that may be analysed computationally to reveal patterns, trends and associations especially relating to human behaviour and interactions

Internet of things

...the extension of internet connectivity into physical devices and everyday objects. Embedded with electronics, internet connectivity and other forms of hardware these devices can communicate and interact with other over the internet. They can be remotely monitored and controlled.

Fast Data

...the application of big data analytics to smaller data sets in near time or real time in order to solve a problem or create business value. The goal of fast data is to quickly gather and mine data so action can be taken.

Artificial intelligence (AI)

...the creation of intelligent machines that simulate human intelligence: learning, reasoning and self-correction. Increasingly termed as **Augmented Intelligence** to emphasise that the main objective of AI is not to replace humans but support and enhance the capability of people using it.

According to research conducted by the OECD[4] half of all jobs will be affected by automation in the coming years, with 14 per cent being highly automatable and another 32 per cent of jobs having between 50 per cent and 70 per cent of their tasks subject to automation. Research carried out by Accenture, McKinsey Global and PWC also found that only a small percentage of jobs are likely to be replaced entirely by Artificial Intelligence (AI). They also agreed that AI will affect about 60

---

[4] Nedelkoska, L. and G. Quintini (2018), 'Automation, skills use and training', *OECD Social, Employment and Migration Working Papers*, No. 202, OECD Publishing, Paris, https://doi.org/10.1787/2e2f4eea-en.

per cent of all jobs as at least one third of the tasks they carry out could be automated.

The same research suggests that, for now, automation is less likely to affect those jobs that require creativity, involve managing or interacting with people, operate in unpredictable environments or are technically difficult or expensive to automate.

60% of jobs will be affected by AI
Source: McKinsey Global

Historically automation has resulted in the creation of new kinds of jobs and there is no indication that this fourth industrial revolution will be any different.

So, while we won't see technology drastically reducing the number of jobs available any losses that do occur are likely to be offset by the number of new jobs created. AI will, however, transform the majority of the jobs that exist today and create new jobs that we don't even know we need yet.

What does this mean for us as business leaders?

Technology will carry on changing the way we work and the way work gets done.

Technology will continue to remove the need for people to do routine, repetitive and rule-based tasks. By taking these tasks away, organisations, and their people, will be able to focus on more valuable activities – the activities that differentiate products and services and make businesses more competitive, resilient and profitable.

And this redistribution of activities means that, in the very near future, jobs will need a different mix of skills. Some of the skills we need now will no longer be necessary. The table below identifies the skills anticipated to be most in demand in the future.

The Future of Work: Job Skills in most Demand

Learning				Adaptable	
Building Rapport	Critical Thinking	Teamwork		Problem Solving	Decision Making
		Collaboration			
Judgement		Planning	Empathy	Creativity	

The increased volume and speed at which data is produced along with the pace of technological change will reduce the shelf life of both knowledge and technology skills – making lifelong learning a prerequisite for everyone. The faster the pace of change the more learning will be required and the more flexible and adaptable people will need to be.

> '1,500 years ago, everybody knew that the Earth was the centre of the universe. 500 years ago, everybody knew that the Earth was flat. And 15 minutes ago, you knew that humans were alone on this planet. Imagine what you'll know tomorrow'.
>
> Agent K, Men in Black.
> (Tommy Lee Jones)

There will of course be more demand for skills to support, improve and create these technologies and there will also be greater requirement for higher level cognitive and analytical skills to analyse the data and outputs they produce.

In the future jobs will also require people to spend more time doing things technology can't do, like managing people, innovating and communicating with customers. For instance the collection and analysis of data can be automated but the factors and fluidity involved in critical thinking and decision-making cannot.

Technology can only communicate on a basic level - it can't empathise, build rapport or establish trust, all of which are vital for effective teamwork and successful collaboration. This level of emotional intelligence cannot be automated but is essential for engaging both employees and customers.

Is technology holding us back?

Tension:
The state of being stretched tight
Mental or emotional strain

Having people with the right skills will be an essential ingredient for successful automation and AI. Many of these skills are, however, in short supply[5] and we can expect increasing demand to put further strain on these already stretched resources. As skills are developed over time through experience and practice, filling the gap will not happen overnight.

The following factors will continue to create tension in the workplace, testing the availability and learning of these vital skills:

---

[5] Department for Education *Employer Skills Survey 2017*

- Resistance to change - one of the major contributors to failure in this case will be fueled by fears over job security and concerns about monitoring and surveillance.

- Isolation - globalisation and the ability to connect anytime and on any device means that more people can and will work remotely, which will make it harder to collaborate and develop communication and team-working skills. People don't want technology to replace the personal connections and interactions they have at work either.[6]

- Fast Communication – the preference for frequent electronic communication will continue to impact on the development of interpersonal skills, reducing the content and quality of conversation and non-verbal communication.

- Structure - work will be organised, structured and done in new ways, increasingly carried out by different types of workers, from employees to freelancers, contractors and gig workers, redefining the Leadership role and making teamwork and meaningful collaboration more challenging.

- Data overload – people may be overwhelmed by the availability and volume of data and information and will need support to keep up with the pace and continuous pressure to change.

These same issues will also present a risk to workers' engagement and mental health.

We know a highly engaged workforce delivers better business performance and positively impacts the bottom line. We also know that high levels of engagement will only be sustained when matched with good levels of mental health and wellbeing.

---

[6] PwC Consumer Intelligence Series: *Tech at Work 2018*

Demo?

As long as our work gives us a sense of purpose, provides financial security, independence and the opportunity to socialise it will remain a key factor in engagement and in preventing physical and mental health problems. See Sustainable Engagement Table below.

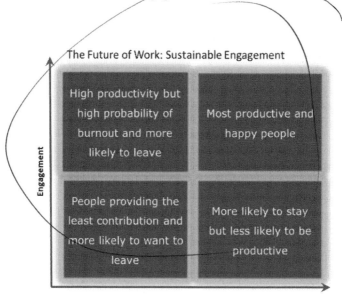

Leaders will need to manage all of these tensions to successfully take advantage of future technologies - this means investing in people as well as technology. To achieve this they will have to continually assess how technology fits their plans, existing job roles, structures, and ways of working. And foster a working culture where people care about each other, a culture that involves every part of the organisation and supports people to develop the skills necessary in this never ending cycle of change.

What's the solution?

It is what humans do, not the technology, that will add value to organisations in the future. To deliver this added value leaders will need to build teams and organisations with the soft skills necessary to constantly learn, adapt and change. That means creating new ways of working and new ways of developing the skills organisations need.

Collaboration is a catalyst for developing the skills essential to the future of work. It goes hand in hand with teamwork, building trust and a sense of belonging that will overcome feelings of isolation, improving the flow and quality of communication and boosting learning, innovation and efficiency. It is also an important factor in building levels of employee engagement and wellbeing which in turn improves an organisation's ability to attract and retain employees.

Collaboration is at the core of the solutions-based process Design Thinking and that's why it could be an effective Leadership approach for the future. Design Thinking brings people together to focus on creating solutions rather than solving problems. And because it puts the customer at its heart the process is more likely to create solutions, products and services that differentiate your business and benefit your bottom line.

The Stanford d.school process, on the following page, takes people (and their different views and perspectives) through 5 different modes of thinking in order to identify and create the best service, product or solution to a problem. The process lends itself to challenging assumptions and exploring new pathways and ideas.

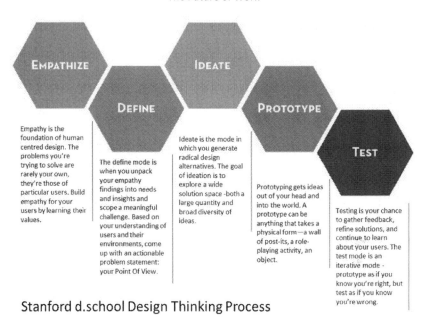

Stanford d.school Design Thinking Process

By employing the principles of Design Thinking in everyday activities leaders will give practical opportunities for people to learn, experience and develop the skills they need for the future of work including:

- Empathy – this is a particular strength of Design Thinking as each step of the process puts the needs of the customer first. Understanding others, their perspectives and experiences, finding out what is important to them and what they want, enables people to build stronger and more trusting relationships.
- Teamwork and Collaboration – the issue and the solution is defined by the team in Design Thinking. People feel 'safe' to make mistakes, give feedback and manage differences and disagreements when they have a shared understanding and goal.

- Critical Thinking and Problem Solving – in Design Thinking people proactively ask questions, evaluate findings and arguments, in order to get to the root of a problem
- Creativity – instead of doing what has always been done, Design Thinking encourages people to be curious, to think outside of the box and to learn from, explore and build on other people's ideas.
- Adaptability – Design Thinking is an iterative process. Feedback, flexibility and adaptability is vital if you are to finish with the best possible outcome.

Where to start?

Technology is changing work, augmenting what people do, enabling them to be more capable and productive. Humans and being human will remain critical for organisation success in the future. Leaders must invest in and take better care of their people in order to take full advantage of the opportunities that technology brings.

I. Identify your priorities:

In order to care for your people properly you will need to understand what they want and how they feel. You want to know if they're motivated and engaged – as that is what affects job performance, customer service, the ability to learn and innovate and loyalty. Only when you know how people feel will you understand your strengths, problems and what to do about them.

You'll also need to understand people's attitudes and behaviour toward technology. What will motivate, or hinder, people from learning new technologies? What will encourage them to adapt and change the way they work in order to use them effectively?

An employee survey is an efficient way to gather feedback from everyone and will enable you to:

- Understand how people feel
- Find out how people feel about technologies, plans and strategies for change
- Measure how technologies and plans have impacted employee loyalty and performance
- Collect and use feedback to implement (more) effective plans
- Identify and address concerns and problems before they escalate
- Better manage change in the future
- Identify where to focus.

This is the first step in any Design Thinking process and will enable you to develop understanding and build empathy with your employees and workers.

Gathering feedback will help you identify your strengths, problems and priorities but once you have that information the way you use it becomes far more important. So don't rely on electronic communication to feedback the findings – this is a valuable and logical opportunity to engage people in another stage of Design Thinking.

The next step is to identify an opportunity or problem that needs solving and bring people together, using face to face meetings and, or collaborative technologies to create a solution.

II. Take small steps toward the future of work

Leaders who focus on building collaborative organisations will be better equipped to take advantage of technology. Here's some practical advice to help you on your journey toward a collaborative, Design Thinking workplace:

1. Start now – the future of work is now and you can't afford not to take action.

2. Start small – use employee feedback to identify something you can deliver in the short term, as an opportunity to practise new skills and behaviours, and to build momentum for change.

3. Use technologies to encourage and support collaborative working across functions and teams. But be aware of the potential pitfalls and problems technology may bring.

4. Tell people what is expected of them in terms of their role and the overall goal so they can focus on collaborating rather than competing with each other.

5. Be a role model for the behaviours that you want to see.

6. Communicate often. Create opportunities and make time for *personal* interaction so you get to know your people, their likes, dislikes, interests and fears, and your people get to know and trust you.

7. Acknowledge and appreciate people when they demonstrate the behaviours that you want.

8. Work flexibly. You can begin the Design Thinking process at any point as innovative solutions don't just come at the end of the process. You can also move back and forward and jump to different stages - just do what makes most sense for your people and your particular goal.

9. Don't expect results straightaway. Give people time to test, understand and apply these new ideas and ways of thinking. Over time and consistently supported they will embed and start to become the new norm.

10. Reinforce the application of new ways of working, new skills and behaviours - give some thought to how you can measure and communicate successes. You could track the number of projects using them and what they achieve. Or carry out an employee survey to measure and benchmark progress.

Summary

The future of work will be defined by technology but as you move forward stay mindful of the advantages and potential problems it brings. Invest equally in technology and in developing the skills and behaviours you need to support it.

Use technologies to build a collaborative culture that puts people at its heart. Above all keep your organisation 'human'. The 'human touch' is what will enable you to innovate and differentiate your products and services.

About the author

Michelle Bailey BA MCIPD
www.peopleessentials.co.uk

Michelle Bailey is the founder of People Essentials the engagement and people specialists. Michelle has worked for more than 25 years in Human Resources across a range of sectors including IT, engineering, logistics, construction, retail and professional services. Michelle has a diverse range of experience. Her membership of Engage for Success[7] and as a committee member of the Thames Valley Branch of the Chartered Institute of Personnel and Development provides her access to the latest thinking and best practice on organisation development and people matters.

Established in 2010 People Essentials is a specialist Human Resources consultancy that helps organisations create workplaces that attract and motivate people to embrace change and perform their best.

People Essentials have developed their own survey platform to provide valuable business insight, and a framework for boosting engagement, wellbeing and productivity, as well as the support to take action.

---

[7] Engage for Success is a voluntary movement promoting employee engagement as a better way to work

Managing employee conflict in tomorrow's workplace

By Marc Reid

Introduction

As a mediator, I am a naturally optimistic person. It goes with the job. You need to maintain a belief that the clients you work with can overcome their conflict despite their own scepticism and the lack of conviction of those around them. It goes against the grain therefore to begin my chapter with what appears a rather bleak assertion:

CONFLICT IS INEVITABLE

Look back in history though and it is clear people have forever been in conflict. When faced with a threat, if peaceful means of resolution fail, we fall into conflict. It is part of being human, it is part of our society and will always remain so.

Our workplace can be viewed as a microcosm of our society and so I'm afraid we must conclude that conflict is inevitable in the workplace now and in the future. But that's not bad news, or even good news (unless you are a professional mediator), it is simply a fact, so we need to ensure we are best placed to mitigate any potential negative impacts.

In this chapter I'll look at where the potential for future workplace conflict might arise and how we can best equip our workplaces to manage it effectively.

Key societal and workplace trends

Our future world of work won't evolve in a vacuum, it will be determined by how society develops. I've selected three societal trends and consider how they manifest themselves in the workplace of tomorrow. I've focused on three where I believe the potential for resulting conflict is considerable.

Societal Trend	Associated Workplace Trend
Technology	Remote working, increased automation, 'always on' mentality
Generational Divide	Multiple generations in the workforce, growing proportion of millennials
Loss of Respect	Growing workplace incivility

Technology

Microsoft founder, Bill Gates, once said "We're changing the world with technology" and there can be little doubt technology has brought dramatic change in recent years. Today's smartphones have several thousand times more computing power than the NASA computers which put a man on the moon. Technology has driven social change, facilitating globalisation and universal connectivity.

In terms of work, technology has revolutionised the 'workplace' itself. In the past, you travelled to work, sat at your desk in an office block from 9-5, and travelled home. Now your workplace could be your bedroom, the local coffee shop or the 18.10 from Paddington. Teams that used to sit in close proximity may now be located in different countries and potentially never meet face to face. For this new virtual workplace to be effective the critical factor is good communication.

Technology facilitates this with a wide and ever-evolving range of options from old favourites like email and telephone to 'new kids' like instant messaging, video conferencing and social media.

With all this communication surely that means less conflict in the future? That's not how I see it. Two of the major risks I see are as follows:

1. **Less face-to-face increases miscommunication potential**. When we speak to someone in person we convey our meaning not only through the words we use but the tone of voice and our associated body language. Reading an email or text limits our ability to understand how the person intended the words to come across.

   I have seen many cases in mediations where the conflict has escalated as someone has chosen to interpret written words in a way that the sender didn't intend. So if remote working and virtual teams become the future norm, the potential for miscommunication and consequential conflict will increase.

2. **Expectation of constant availability**. I still remember the shock the first time I received an email from a work colleague who I knew to be on holiday. She took great delight in using her new Blackberry to reply to emails, and letting everyone know she was doing so whilst sunning herself on the beach.

   Fast forward a few years and we live in an 'always on' society. Our phones deliver our emails, messages, social media posts and sometimes even a phone call. In many workplaces there is an expectation that you should be contactable. Inevitably, for some this can impact negatively on their mental health. Not being able to escape from work leads to stress, and stressed people are more prone to finding themselves in conflict. I've worked with mediation participants who have made assumptions and jumped to conclusions due to being in a stressed state, causing them to behave and respond in a way they would not have done normally.

Generational Divide

In the past society has taken for granted that our children will be better off than we were. In other words the expectation is for a sustained increase in living standards. Yet recent figures show that for the first time this century this will not be the case. Our children will be worse off than we were at the same age.[8] This is the plight of the Millennial generation, those born between 1981-2000. We have seen clear indications of this in the UK with rapidly increasing house prices and slow wage growth, compounded by poor pension prospects and the burden of student debt. It has led to resentment towards older generations and a shift in values away from those that have driven the Baby Boomers and Generation X's (i.e. born mid 1940s – mid 1970s).

Inevitably this has consequences for the workplace as Millennials will be an increasing proportion of the working population. By 2025 it is estimated that Millennials will make up as much as 75% of the US workforce.[9] But how does this increase the conflict risk as surely we have had different generations in the workforce before? The issue is that what engages and motivates Millennials may be quite different from what the drivers are for previous generations. For instance it has been suggested that Millennials have stronger focus on the group, and collaboration more than the individual, and place greater emphasis on

---

[8] Millennials poorer than previous generations – Financial Times, 23 February, 2018

[9] Millennials and the Future of Corporate America – Brookings Governance Studies, May 2014

social focus and corporate responsibility.[10] Moreover, communication itself is different for Millennials; they have grown up with digital communication and prefer quick, brief communication like text and instant messaging rather than face-to-face or phone calls, which would be the preference of earlier generations.[11]

I want to avoid over generalisation as viewing people as a label as opposed to an individual is in itself a direct path towards conflict! But what is certainly true is that a key reason for people finding themselves in conflict is an inability to see the perspective of the other person. As such, if we have generations in the workforce which are predisposed to having significantly different value sets, it creates fertile ground for potential conflict.

Loss of Respect

In recent years events such as the financial crisis, the parliamentary expenses scandal, the Stephen Lawrence case and the Hillsborough disaster have undermined the public's confidence and respect in previously highly regarded people and organisations like politicians and the police.

At the same time we have seen a growth in incivility in society as this lack of respect appears to have broadened to our fellow humans. Social media has fuelled this growth, allowing people to be uncivil whilst hiding behind a Twitter or Facebook profile. But it has also translated into face-to-face situations. Research in America[12] highlighted that in 2018, 84% of Americans had experienced incivility and the number of average uncivil encounters per week was over 10. You might expect this to be mainly online but actually around half

---

[10] Workforce 2020: What you need to know now – Forbes, 5 May, 2016
[11] Marketing and Selling to Millennials – The Center for Generational Kinetics
[12] Civility in America 2018 – Weber Shandwick

were in person, and most alarmingly the rate had doubled in only two years.

Inevitably the loss of respect and growth of incivility is reflected in our workplaces. Research indicates that incidents of employees treating colleagues rudely have increased significantly over the past decade.[13] of survey respondents in 1998 reported being treated rudely by colleagues at least once a month. The same figure for the 2016 survey was 62%. As we look to the future it is difficult to see the trend changing. Increased stress levels and less face-to-face contact will only exacerbate the potential for incivility and hence the likelihood of resulting in conflict between employees.

What can managers do?

We have seen that the potential for relationship conflict between employees in our future world of work is considerable, and, I would argue, significantly greater than exists today. It is imperative therefore that managers have strategies to address this risk. Sadly the approach of many managers is to avoid relationship conflict as it is difficult to deal with. They therefore miss the chance to nip conflict in the bud, and as a result it escalates and causes harm to the people involved, the wider team and potentially the whole organisation.

My solution for managers is to take a proactive tiered approach which can be summarised as the 3 P's:

---

[13] The hidden toll of workplace incivility – McKinsey Quarterly, Dec 2016

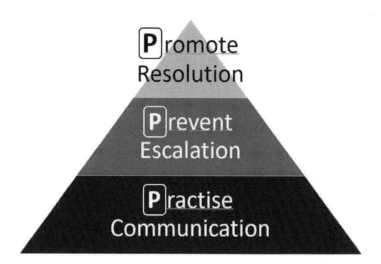

I will look at each of these and propose simple tools that can assist managers.

Practise communication

To misquote Tony Blair, the manager wanting to minimise conflict in their team should have 3 priorities 'Communication. Communication. Communication'. Conflict struggles to grow in an environment where people have open, honest and respectful conversations. The manager's job is twofold in this respect. First they must lead by example and adopt this communication style with their team members. Secondly they need to train their employees to feel confident enough to communicate in this way with their colleagues.

If employees are empowered in this way they will be able to resolve any issues they have with each other by talking about it and finding a way forward. It is not easy though and won't come naturally to most. Our normal reaction to potential conflict is to avoid or get someone else to sort it out. This is why training is important: so employees learn to have the conversation, and develop ways to communicate concerns effectively. An example of this is HEAR, an assertive communication tool that enables the employee to get their point across clearly but without triggering a defensive response.

HEAR	Action	Example
H appening	State clearly what the problem behaviour is	*When you interrupted me in the meeting yesterday...*
E ffect	Describe how their behaviour has impacted on you	*I felt frustrated and undermined...*
A cknowledge	Show you see the situation from their perspective	*I know you were keen to make your point and we didn't have much time left...*
R equest	State what you would like to happen instead	*But next time I'd prefer if you could let me finish before jumping in.*

Prevent escalation

Inevitably some people may not be able to resolve issues between themselves and the situation will escalate to the point that the manager will need to support those involved. The key to avoiding escalation is to act early. The earlier conflict is addressed the easier it is to resolve.

In order to take action the manager will need to:

a) Identify the red flags that could indicate conflict.
b) Understand the options available to address it.
c) Act with confidence and competence to resolve it.

The manager will not automatically know how to do this. Training is essential to know how to identify issues and how to go about dealing with them. Managers will often be able to address issues themselves with a 'quiet word' or having a 'difficult conversation' with one or both of those involved. One of the key decisions will be whether the issue requires a formal or informal approach. The table below highlights the types of issue, and their features, that each approach might be used for:

Formal	Informal
Types of issue	**Types of issue**
• Where absolute right / wrong is needed e.g. potential criminal activity • Clear evidence of injustice e.g. discrimination / harassment • Clear disciplinary matter e.g. breaches of policy • Major power / status differential between participants	• Communication issues • Personality clashes • Perceived discrimination / harassment • Differences in working style • Inappropriate use of power / status • Rebuild relationships after formal process
Features	**Features**
• Complaint on record • Structured investigation • Laid-down timescales • Focus on past and establishing what happened	• Handled confidentially • Informal discussions • Timescale flexible • Focus on underlying issues and how to work in future

Promote Resolution

If despite best efforts the situation escalates further there is a need for third party intervention to resolve the conflict. There are a number of options which could be used and at this point the manager will normally be consulting with Human Resources to decide the best approach to take.

Previously I highlighted where we might see more conflict arising in the future. The common theme for all three is relationship conflict, for which an informal, forward focused approach is more likely to be successful than a backwards looking formal grievance type process - which relies on finding a right / wrong. Workplace mediation is increasingly being used to address relationship conflicts as it enables those involved to find a way forward which works for them both. It is a fast and flexible process which avoids having to involve others, so it can result in a rapid and more satisfactory resolution. The question is often asked – Is this case suitable for mediation? I've designed the tool below to help with this. If you can answer Yes to most of the questions then mediation is likely to be a good option to take.

7 Questions to assess suitability for mediation

M ediation understood	⇒ Have those involved understood what mediation is and indicated they are willing to try it?
E scalation potential	⇒ Does the situation have the potential to escalate and cause more serious damage?
D efinite need to work together	⇒ Is there is a clear business need for those involved to work effectively together going forward?
I ssue not black / white	⇒ Does the situation require an outcome which is not a straightforward right / wrong or yes / no?
A ffecting the business	⇒ If it is not resolved is the conflict likely to have a negative impact on the business?
T ried to resolve themselves	⇒ Have the participants tried to address the issues themselves but now need assistance?
E mployees control the issues	⇒ Are the issues causing the conflict within the control of those involved to resolve?

In summary, our future workplace will be influenced by societal trends that are indicating a greater potential for workplace relationship conflict than has existed in the past. Technology will continue to limit face-to-face contact, the generational divide will make it more difficult to understand someone else's perspective, and the increase in incivility will exacerbate stress levels. All of these factors mean that managers need tools and strategies in place to address conflict. The tiered approach of Practise Communication, Prevent Escalation and Promote Resolution gives the manager a powerful toolkit to deal with future conflict effectively.

About the author

Marc Reid

www.mediation4.co.uk

Marc is an experienced workplace mediator, accredited by CEDR and Civil Mediation Council Registered. He has trained conflict management skills for many years and is author of '*DIY Mediation. The Conflict Resolution Toolkit for HR*' and '*8 Stages of Workplace Conflict*'.

Marc runs Mediation4 which helps organisations manage and resolve workplace conflict. He has mediated a wide range of cases and has also established and run mediation services for a top multinational company.

Marc combines his mediation expertise and knowledge with 25 years' experience in senior corporate commercial, HR and general management roles. He also works as Board Director and Lead Mediator with the local community mediation charity and is an active CIPD volunteer.

The search for productivity

Peter Thomson

Where have we come from?

For the last 200 years the predominant model for work has been employment. Work is performed by employees doing jobs in organisations. Whether they are in the public or private sectors, enterprises achieve their results by dividing work into tasks performed by individuals. These jobs are arranged in hierarchical structures so the people at the top can provide direction and the people below can carry out the day-to-day work.

Over the 20th Century the large multinational businesses flourished, encouraged by the belief that there were economies of scale and benefits from standardisation. Production-line work processes were introduced in the name of efficiency, reducing many jobs to routine, repetitive tasks. Frederic Taylor famously introduced 'Scientific Management' in the name of efficiency and was a major influence on work processes for the first half of the century.

By the 1950s there was a realisation that organising work into boring jobs was not ultimately a highly productive process. People were not prepared to be treated like machines, they wanted more meaningful and satisfying work. They even went to the point of sabotaging the production line just to create a bit more interest and excitement. Employers realised that they needed to motivate their workforce and understand how to reward them effectively.

Many new ideas were tried in the second half of the 20th century, designed to improve the output from the workforce. Managers were trained in techniques to 'engage' employees, HR departments focussed on improving the 'quality' of jobs and organisations introduced benefits that helped people feel recognised and rewarded. But all these were still variations on the hierarchical structure with power held at the top of the pyramid.

Things are now changing

As we moved into the 21st Century, it became clear that some of the assumptions about work from the previous decades were rapidly being overtaken by events. Manual labour in factories was being replaced by robots, routine office work was being replaced by computers and many traditional jobs were disappearing altogether as the Internet reached into everyone's lives. From travel agents to insurance brokers, the customer could go directly to an online service. From department stores to small shops, the explosion in Internet shopping has changed the face of the high street.

Yet the predominant pattern of work has still been made up of people performing jobs in exchange for a salary. There has been a small shift towards self-employment as the 'gig economy' starts to take hold, but the inertia that exists in traditional organisations prevails. As we move further into the digital age this is likely to change. Platforms such as Uber are the tip of an iceberg in the world of work. They have shown that there is an alternative model which can be very effective and doesn't involve the overheads of a corporate structure.

We are measuring the wrong things

The problem with conventional employment is the reward system. People are paid by the hour. Even if they are not paid overtime for extra hours, they have a salary which is related to the time they spend working. Part-time workers are paid less than full-time employees on a pro-rata basis. The contract of employment states the hours someone works and the salary they earn. It doesn't say anything about what they produce.

In this environment people who work long hours are seen to be the loyal, hard-working employees. They are the dedicated ones who put in the effort to keep the business going. They get promoted to senior positions as a reward. On the other hand, people who leave work early to get home are seen to be less valuable. They obviously have other priorities, like family pressures, which divert their efforts. As a result, we end up with long-hours work cultures and associated increases in stress levels.

But rewarding people for effort bears no relation to productivity. In fact it is the reverse. If we have two employees doing the same job to the same quality and one gets it done in a shorter time, by definition they are more productive. The person who takes longer is less efficient, yet we often see them as the better employee. Why is this?

The answer is that we are measuring the wrong things. We measure effort, or input, in hours, rather than measuring what is produced as output. Yet all jobs are created to achieve a result of some sort. So if we measure that, and reward people for actually doing work, not just making an effort, we will encourage productivity. The problem is that many managers struggle to define the output from their employees and resort to input measures as the easy option.

It's now becoming more visible

Take part-time work as an example. Our conventional payment systems reward people pro-rata. So the person who works half-time gets 50 percent of the salary of the full-time employee. Yet there is ample evidence to show that people do not produce results equally per hour in most jobs. They slow down as they get tired, or they stretch the work out to fill the time available.

It is now quite common for parents, returning from parental leave, to request to work part- time. Managers who do not want to lose experienced employees are usually willing to say 'yes' and will welcome them back perhaps for a four-day week. The boss may well ask the individual to see how much of their job they can still get done in the shorter time. Then they review progress after a few months. At this review it's quite likely that managers discover most, if not all, of the 'full-time' results are still being achieved.

The employee has reacted positively to being able to take more time with their family and has been more motivated. They have probably cut out some time-wasting activities associated with the old way of working. And they have adjusted the way they work to make best use of the time available. The manager is happy because he or she has an effective employee and is now only paying four-fifths of the salary.

The problem comes at salary review time and the employee works out that they are being paid less than 'full-time' colleagues for doing the same job. Yet they are clearly doing it in a more productive way. If they don't get rewarded equally they can be tempted to look around for a fairer system and take their talents elsewhere.

How can it be done differently?

An alternative to jobs and salaries is self-employment. By definition, someone running their own business is paid by results. The Uber driver is paid to take the passenger from A to B. But when conventional views of work are applied there is a problem. How can you apply legislation such as minimum wage regulations, expressed in hourly pay units, to someone who is paid for output?

Small companies have some chance of measuring people on the impact they have on the business as a whole but as they grow this becomes more complicated. Take the example of two people who run their own replacement windows business. They get appointments, visit the customer, estimate price and sell the job. They measure up and make some drawings, then go back to the workshop and make the new windows. Finally they go and install them. They also do their own invoicing and accounts paperwork, and take messages from customers on their mobile phones amongst all of the above. They do five windows a week.

They run this business successfully and soon the business starts to grow. First they recruit a PA to take phone calls, do the invoicing and organise things for them, at a much cheaper hourly rate than them. As business expands they buy a new faster machine for making the windows and recruit a sales person to bring in more work. Before long they add a surveyor to help with the measuring up, and several production people to make the windows in a production line system. This needs a production planner / project manager, and a quality controller. Soon they also need a finance person, and a marketing/social media person, an IT person and a part time HR person.

By now they have 40 people and they are full time managers of the business. They produce 80 windows a week and are making a lot more money than they did when they first started on five windows a week. So it looks like a thriving, productive business. But is it really? It may appear that productivity has increased but in fact it's less productive than when they started. The two of them produced five windows a week. So with 40 employees they should be producing 100 a week to keep the same level of productivity per person. At the new rate of 80 per week productivity has actually gone down. Why is this?

Clearly this is because the accounts person doesn't make windows, neither does the IT person or the production controller, so it's almost a miracle that the small number of people in the factory can make 80 a week. They need those economies of scale in order to keep up with doing 80. Similarly, the invoice processer does the invoices much faster than the original two people used to, and the sales person is selling 80 per week as opposed to their original 5, which is very efficient and impressive. So each person has achieved economies of scale by specialising.

But the operation as a whole hasn't shown economies of scale. Each part is more efficient, but overall it's not. And the bigger the organisation the worse the potential problem. So let's look at why:

Reason 1 – Losses between departments

There's a cost every time a sales person explains to the designers what they have sold. It takes time even when it is totally clear and takes much more time when there are questions and misunderstandings. There's another cost when the designers have to take time to explain to production what they want to have made, even if it is an accurate reflection of the customer needs. All this adds cost to fulfilling an order and runs the risk of expensive mistakes happening because of poor communication between people in the decision process.

When the original two owners were doing everything they didn't have any of these losses. It was in their heads, and almost impossible for them to sell something that they couldn't make. These losses would be bad enough if it was just communication time, but often you have to actually employ a full-time person to be the link; like production control or project management, or customer service, or technical support. Which brings us to the second reason.

Reason 2 – The inefficiency of fixed roles

As a business grows it is quite normal that the jobs it performs have to be split up. The more it grows the more divided the jobs become. In the case of an accounts department in a larger enterprise, there may be different people responsible for the different ledgers (purchase, sales and nominal). The role of an individual is confined to the role specified in their contract of employment.

So if, using the example above, the company has limited purchasing in a period then what does the purchase ledger clerk do? Their skills are specific and not transferable. Their contract of employment defines the hours and the skills they are expected to bring. What can they reasonably be expected to do when there is no work in their domain? The answer usually is to slow down. The people are just victims of the system, usually doing the best they can within their own control. But it is harder to remain motivated in a divided-up world.

Reason 3 – Lack of ownership

When you only do part of the job, say the design, you can blame any problems on the person who sold it or the person who made it. And even if you're not the blaming kind, you just don't feel that you OWN that product. (The accounts clerk may have absolutely no idea as to what the business does and the machine operator may have little idea where the part they are making is likely to end up.)

The production people often never meet the customer, so there's less incentive to make it great, and less understanding of exactly what that person wants, or why. They can easily feel as if sales and design and finance are deliberately trying to make their job harder. Of course they're not really, but their performance measures are probably forcing them to behave in that way.

In some big companies it's really hard to care even if you want to. You end up spending 90 percent of your time fighting the system, just trying to get a better deal for the customer, or to reduce the stupid wastes of time and money that go on. Meetings, politics, feuds and games, all add to the cost. If only the system could be designed so that everyone was pulling in the same direction.

Reason 4 – Carrying the weak ones

Research has shown that in a tug of war you can measure the force that people exert on the rope and come up with an interesting result. If you measure one against one, and then measure the force from eight against eight you find they are only pulling with five times the force, not eight (The Ringelmann effect 1913). This is partly because of communication losses but also because you can pull with less effort and nobody will know. So because some people perform better than others, when you make organisations larger you don't get the expected output from everyone, especially when the system is already frustrating for the people involved.

There is less incentive because individual performance isn't visible. The people in Ringelmann's experiment weren't bad people, it was just how they respond to the situation they were in. We work better if we can see the results of our own individual performance. It is also true that a small minority of people can and will get away with deliberately doing less work. It's been over 100 years since Max Ringelmann carried out his famous experiment yet we have never applied this learning to our Organisational Designs.

Where do we go from here?

When there were just two people making windows it was easy. Now with 80 people in specialised roles producing windows, or anything else for that matter, how can you get everyone to do everything. Get everyone to do a bit of selling, a bit of designing, a bit of making, a bit of finance and quality control – everything. It seems impossible, but it can be done. Instead of expanding by making jobs narrower, just add more of the multi-skilled ones.

If our 80 person complicated company of specialised people converted to 40 pairs of people, each pair doing everything, productivity would improve dramatically. Each pair would do five windows a week, and probably enjoy doing it, producing 100 instead of 80. It's going to be difficult to design and build a skyscraper or manufacture a car using self-employed people, but there are many situations where the approach to work design can minimise the problems caused by specialisation.

So in the interest of productivity we are likely to see many more small businesses in the future, without the overhead burdens associated with specialist departments. Technology will allow people to perform work directly for customers and be paid for their services not for their time. And there will be a revolution in the way work is distributed within companies, creating multi-skilled jobs for employees with broad responsibilities, buying in specialist support only when needed.

What does this mean for leaders?

If we want to improve the productivity of an organisation as a whole, we have to find a way that individuals can see the effect they have on the whole. As long as they are being rewarded on a narrow slice of the business they will not be working towards the overall corporate goal. Internal departments will be fighting to get a higher share of the overhead budget, not trying to reduce their costs in the interest of the bigger bottom line. Specialist groups will be producing arguments why their discipline is needed to justify employing expensive experts. So how can we expose each individual person to the clear light of measurement, so they know how much effect they have on the money for the whole business?

The solution is to genuinely empower people. Leaders in the future will need to do more than just pay lip-service to the concept of delegating power. They will actually need to trust people to make decisions and let them get on with doing the work. This will mean removing many management controls, relying instead on measuring people on their results. No longer will the most effective leaders be those with the biggest empires. To meet the challenges of the 21st Century it will be those with the most productive workforce and the most agile organisation.

About the author

Peter Thomson

www.wisework.co.uk

Peter is an expert on the changing world of work and its impact on organisations, leadership and management. He regularly speaks on this topic at conferences and has worked with many groups of senior managers to inspire them to change their organisational culture. He is a director of the Future Work Forum, a 'think tank' of leading consultants.

He headed up the HR function for Digital Equipment for Northern Europe for 18 years leading up to the dawn of the Internet. On leaving DEC, Peter became a Visiting Fellow at Henley Business School and for 16 years he studied the changing patterns of work and the leadership implications of these trends. At the same time he formed Wisework Ltd, now a leading consultancy in the field of smart working.

Peter is co-author, with Alison Maitland, of the business bestseller 'Future Work'. He is also editor of a new book 'Conquering Digital Overload'. This book shows leaders how to change their organisation culture to reduce the stresses of 'always-on' working patterns.

As a consultant and coach, Peter works with leadership teams and individuals to help them gain the maximum business benefit from new working practices. As a writer and researcher he is fascinated by the evolving role of leadership and management as we move into the 'Gig Economy'.

Key Line Management Skills for the Future

Heather Mills

When we talk about what effective management will look like in the future, we need to first ask ourselves a few questions. What will the workforce of the future look like? What will the workplace look like? And how are managers doing right now?

What will the workforce of the future look like?

Ageing population

Over the last 30 years, the employment rate for people aged 50 to 64 has increased by 14%, while the employment rate for the 65+ age group has doubled (DWP, 2015). About 1/3 of the UK's workforce is now over the age of 50 (ONS, Labour market projections 2006-2020). Older workers come with a wealth of experience but they may also have caring responsibilities and age-related health issues which need to be considered.

5-generation workplace

Generation Z is starting to join the workforce, giving a 5th generation to manage and, of course, each new generation has different expectations from work than the last.

5 GENERATIONS IN THE WORKPLACE

TRADITIONALISTS

Born before 1943
Like authority and hierarchy
Hardworking and loyal
Slower to adopt technology
Make do

BABY BOOMERS

Born 1943-1964
Value instructor led courses
Expect deference to experience
Workaholics
More reserved in communication

GENERATION X

Born 1965-1976,
Like hands-off management
Work hard
Want work-life balance

MILLENNIALS

Born 1977-1997
Want meaningful work
Technology savvy
Goal and results orientated
Want to be coached

GENERATION Z

Born 1977 onwards
Digital savvy
Used to change
Wants human contact
Want regular feedback

Technological changes

It is widely accepted that technology will become embedded into everything we do in the workplace. Artificial Intelligence is being used more and more. Some jobs may be replaced by technology, and some may increase, such as those requiring creativity or emotional intelligence.

Gender and racial equality

High on the agenda currently is the topic of equality, in particular gender and racial equality, going beyond Equal Pay for equal work, to considering the percentage difference between average hourly earnings for men and women or ethnic minorities and their white peers. These comparisons highlight differences between starting salaries and pay progression, for example, which can be investigated and addressed. If this stays on the agenda, and it is likely to, the future should see a more diverse workforce in all roles of the organisation.

Contract types

We have seen a lot of interest in different contract types in recent years, from directly employed, to zero hours contracts, to umbrella companies, to contractors, to agency workers. This is expected to continue in the future, when workforces may be made up of less directly employed staff and an overall more varied employment status.

What will the workplace of the future look like?

Remote working is on the rise, with three quarters of the world working remotely at least once per week. Automatic Inc. for example, a billion-dollar company whose CEO created WordPress, exists without any company offices and does not use email for internal communication, instead using a blog theme. It is proving to be an effective way of controlling costs and recruiting and retaining the best talent where they are, without asking them to move nearer to the company.

Just as no-one could predict what would happen in the last 10-20 years, nor can they predict what is going to happen in the next. What is certain is that that we live in changing times. Managers need to communicate effectively to weather and exploit the changes.

How are management doing right now?

There is a strong business case for better management skills in terms of increased employee engagement, improved staff health and wellbeing, and better individual and consequently organisational performance.   And there are undoubtedly good managers out there. Despite this, management performance is mixed.

The CIPD Health and Wellbeing Survey 2019 identified Mental Ill Health and Stress as the top 2 causes of long term absence and cites 'management style' as one of the top 3 causes of stress related absence.

The results of a survey of the UK's largest employer, the NHS, highlighted issues with equality, diversity and inclusion, and bullying and harassment (including 13% of staff reporting experiencing this from managers). Source: The NHS Staff Survey 2018

In 25 years as an HR professional, I have lost count of the number of managers who have told me that their staff are no good, but have never effectively communicated with them. Likewise, how often staff have ended up in formal procedures when a quiet word from the manager at the start would have nipped an issue in the bud.

Acas says 'Even minor problems can develop into grievances or disputes if they're not dealt with quickly and effectively.' But it's often down to management how issues are handled and, Acas says, 'where an issue turns into a problem, a positive result can be achieved through early and informal intervention' i.e. the manager having a quiet word with the staff involved.

Often I get contacted by managers. Their staff member is in their probation period. My staff member is not working out, they tell me, they'll have to go. I say, have you spoken to them? No. Did you provide a job description? No. A job description, induction and then regular support would save losing a potentially good employee and save the time and cost of recruiting another.

Another example is the manager who says they need to discipline their staff member for lateness. I ask, have you spoken to them? Have you asked them if they have trouble getting in on time? Do they need to amend their start time? Have you explained why it is important to the service? Have you given them a chance to improve? No. Again, time and management effort could be saved with a quick chat to find out if there's a problem and resolve it. This could save a small problem developing into a bigger one, and causing a breakdown in the relationship between the manager and staff, and affecting the person's motivation at work.

Why are some managers failing?

- Often managers are promoted without having the appropriate skills.
- They are not trained how to manage their staff. It is often assumed that they can.

- If you've applied for a management role, it is hard to admit that you need management training.
- Some managers are reluctant to have difficult conversations with staff because of how staff will react.
- They are under pressure to meet targets and deadlines and have conflicting priorities and insufficient time.
- The culture of the organisation does not encourage good management.
- A lack of good role models.

Key Line Management skills for the future

We have discussed the future diversity of the workforce in terms of age groups, gender, race, and contract type. If managers are truly going to get to grips with this diversity, they will have to get to know the individuals that they manage, build rapport, find out how each of them ticks, what their needs are, and work out how to get them working together as a team towards meeting goals. The only way to do this is to take the time to talk to each of them regularly and to listen to what they have to say.

In particular, Millennials and Generation Z are looking for coaching, mentoring and regular feedback. Managers must learn to provide constructive corrective critical feedback and praise on a regular basis in order to keep these staff engaged. Marjory's chapter on Feedback shows how to do this well.

Technology is being integrated into everything we do at work, but managers would be wise not to think that electronic communication can replace human interaction. It must be remembered that not all generations were born into a technological world and many want more human contact. Millennials and Generation Z, despite growing up with technology, demonstrate a desire to come into the office and spend time with other humans. Technology cannot replace the human touch and managers need to ensure that they communicate with staff face-to-face on a regular basis. Not only that, e-communication is open to misinterpretation which can lead to people not knowing what their goals are, or to workplace conflict. We know that body language, tone and facial expression all contribute to how the overall message is received and understood.

If the trend for remote working continues, it will be down to managers to find new ways of ensuring meaningful human connections in a virtual culture and world. They can do this by creating a culture of communication, with planned face-to-face and virtual meetings with the manager and the staff, being a good role model, encouraging staff to meet with, get to know and learn from each other, all on a regular basis.

Although it is not across the board, recent reports have cited 'management style' as a significant cause of stress, and accused a percentage of managers of bullying and harassment, and of not promoting equality, diversity and inclusion. Under pressure, it is easy for bad emotions to drive us. Managers need to be aware of their own communication styles and address any negativity. Is their communication style aggressive or confrontational? Or compassionate and supportive? Does it promote goodwill, positivity, raise morale, is it authentic, does it engage staff, does it make staff feel valued? The IIP Employee Sentiment Research 2019 says that half of UK workers will be looking for a new job in 2019 and that 'humans want to be engaged in meaningful relationships, feel valued and useful'. Managers need to find a way to communicate that to staff.

There are many writers on the subject of good management with many different views, but at the end of the day the quality of management and how the workforce is managed is seen as key to improving productivity and the experience of work. Managers need to spend time with their staff, get to know them, listen to them, ask their views, what are their strengths/weaknesses, what do they want, tell them what the organisation goals are and the part they can play, help them with training and support and regular feedback, and deal with problems quickly and fairly. Above all, managers will need to communicate the need for flexibility in constant change because that is what the future holds.

Top Tips

1. Make time for talking and listening to your staff – plan regular 1:1s, find a private space, time, and let them discuss self, work and team

2. Consider your communication style – is it supportive? Inclusive? Compassionate?

3. Be sure to include contractors and agency workers and remote workers too

4. Get to know your staff as individuals – you can only do this by talking to them and listening to them

5. Learn how to talk to different generations, genders and races – what makes them tick

6. Create a culture of communication, be a good role model, encourage staff to talk to and learn from each other

7. Don't be afraid to have difficult conversations with staff who are not performing

8. Give staff regular feedback on their performance, good and bad

9. Encourage staff to feedback to you on your management skills

10. Get out from behind technology and talk to people face-to-face

About the author

Heather Mills MA HRM MCIPD

www.ducksouphr.co.uk

Heather Mills spent the earlier part of her career in Oxford, working with the NHS prior to moving to a local Charity. It was in this role that her expertise came into its own and she was charged with setting up the HR Function from scratch and delivering a strategic and operational HR service.

Armed with 25 years in-depth knowledge of human resources, she identified a need for professional HR support for SMEs which would enable them to get on with business whilst ensuring that they complied with employment law and optimised their most valuable resource, their staff.

Duck Soup HR was born and Heather now works with regular and new clients in the private and public sectors.

The Psychology of a Future You that Works

By Jan P. de Jonge

Modern society and modern economies are being commoditised. Processes are becoming more impersonal. We have more touchpoints with our keyboards than times of being in touch with one-another, it seems.

How will humanity cope with the future world of work? Will it embrace the developments? At work, will leaders become more effective at leading and will workers of the future be more engaged and productive? Will we interact with artificial, virtual entities or will we still be engaging the most with people - our colleagues and clients?

Self-awareness will be crucial

Our self-awareness may prove to be crucial in helping us find our way in the future. This is about our ability to understand not only who we are and how we are perceived by the company we work at, but also the presence of this ability in the people that work with you. For instance, strong levels of self-awareness prevent such phenomena as the above-average effect. Some research found that an impossible number of people believe they are above average on some desirable traits, from the mundane ("I'm a better driver than most") to the more profound ("I'm kinder than the average person around me"). In the world of work, leaders and managers of other people have some level of understanding of the way they impact those around them. Many examples exist of how even the strongest leaders have flaws in their self-perceptions, their self-image or self-esteem.

It's part of human instinct to want to plan and to have fear of the future – even if some people plan, and some fear, the future more than others. Often, planning is undertaken with the wrong and unspoken assumption that planning will secure positive outcomes within a given timeframe. The natural fear we have can stand in the way of change. A recent McKinsey Global Survey about innovation and automation at work identified two main factors that influence the extent to which this new technology is adopted in the workplace: resistance from employees (and how that is managed) and, secondly, attracting talent. Of several key factors determining the success of innovation and automation, the most prominent factor is the ability of organisations to build the skills of its workforce; developing and retaining the internal brains of the company as it aims to innovate.

Above any hi-tech, advanced technology, it is the people who are the most important asset in a company; the human factor is the X-factor. Where mindset and people's abilities are paramount.

The UK-based Institute of Directors in a 2019 publication said: "Nobody knows quite where AI will lead us, but we do know that if businesses don't embrace new technologies they won't survive. But many companies don't know where to start or which technologies to embrace. Organisations that try to bite off too much at the start of their Intelligent Automation journey typically fail to realise returns on their investments for two to three years, by which time funding has dried up. Businesses that do not embrace or respond to new technology are often found to lack a mindset that is needed to be able to embrace that technology.

Wellbeing and effectiveness at work

Designing the right workplace is not as straightforward as we may have thought in recent years. Our workplace impacts on our employee wellbeing; most people agree that the quality of our workspace is important to mental health. It also has a direct link with employee productivity and levels of collaboration. In the future, evolving technologies with increasing accuracy enable us to measure the extent to which a certain work environment fits our individual make-up; our personalities and preferences. Some people work well in a group, some need to be left alone. Some of us are highly disciplined, some of us less so.

Whether it be working in analytics, in IT, new tech, sustainable, remotely or virtual, our personalities will still play a huge role in how we live our working lives, our levels of wellbeing and our effectiveness at work.

Your effectiveness will, for instance, still be impacted by the extent to which you either withdraw from networking or seek to stay in touch with people or create new contacts, by whether you act on impulse or postpone decisions, by the ways in which you reflect, learn, exercise and feel good or bad about yourself and seek opportunities to grow and satisfy your curiosity.

Our individual psyches are unique; we are similar perhaps, in many ways, but we all have our single, highly personal identity. This is partly why there is no secret recipe for wellbeing at work – not only are we all different, each organisation has its own unique culture. And just like people, organisations too, are subject to uncertainty, volatility, and changing circumstances that affect the organisational culture.

Still, several characteristics can be identified in organisations that successfully work on wellbeing, and these characteristics are unlikely to disappear in the years to come:

- Staff are involved and feel involved in how the organisation formally approaches wellbeing. Engagement of staff is closely related to wellbeing.

- Senior management champions the approach that is implemented across the entire organisation. The approach is transparent, aspirational, realistic and widely endorsed.

- Job retention practices ensure that guidance and support is available and early familiarisation is embedded in the organisational identity and, for example, its on-boarding. Organisational culture, work-life balance and workloads are topics that are given due attention.

- Employees (including managers) are trained to detect wellbeing issues. They are able to respond more quickly and confidently when needed. This relates to individuals' self-awareness and capacity to 'self-diagnose', and colleagues who may provide initial support.

- Organisations frequently and systematically monitor wellbeing and thus use data that can be compared over time.

- Impartial and expert support can reduce periods of staff non-productivity, especially if this support is available quickly and action-oriented solutions are identified. Those individuals whose wellbeing is at stake are not always as vocal about that as they would wish to be.

Another indication that the human factor will still reign supreme in the future world of work, despite being faced by indomitable change, is illustrated by the fact that people need to feel contented, safe and respected in their work environment. This need applies to today, but it will also apply to our times ahead.

A survey by Indeed.com in 2017 found that 24% of employees in the tech sector within the United States have experienced personal discrimination at their current place of work – 1 in 4. In other words, treating staff well will remain important, however much futuristic technology takes over. Key concepts as diversity, culture and attitude underpin how organisations operate and whether they thrive.

Needed: leaders of the future

So, what kind of leader will be needed in the future? It is highly likely that the leaders of the future will still be leading people, besides systems and processes. A large body of research evidence[14] gives strong support to the following set of ten conclusions about what makes for effective leaders.

1) Effective leaders are nearly always emotionally stable. This emotional stability refers to one of the generally-accepted 'five factors' of personality: people who possess higher levels of this emotional stability are more likely to feel confident, feel sure of themselves, and are less prone to worrying or self-doubt. These leaders tend to be better at self-regulation, controlling any disruptive emotions and impulses. They adapt. This bears on trustworthiness, integrity and comfort with ambiguity.

2) They are conscientious, in the sense that these leaders are more likely to work hard and smart, show self-discipline, act dutifully and aim for achievement. They are organised; they plan things.

3) People in leadership roles are willing to learn to behave as if they were extroverted, even if they are not. Introverts seem to be at a disadvantage when it comes to being given leadership opportunities and this dynamic gets more pronounced as leadership seniority increases. In the future, approaches and programmes may be designed to help leaders work around this personality characteristic, whereby

---

[14] Examples of research can be requested from the author of this chapter.

the level of introversion of a leader possibly becomes less of a potential hurdle.

4) Effective leaders, of today and in the future, are (within reason) open to new experiences in the context of their business and beyond. Ample research indicates that leaders (from SMEs to presidents) are often more successful when they have broader interests and embrace the complex, ambiguous and subtle.

5) Research into effective leadership suggests that good leaders need to be agreeable at times – but not invariably so. They have an optimistic view of other people and tend to get along with others. They are helpful, respectful and willing to compromise, and they believe that others are basically trustworthy. At the same time, and importantly, they are able to hold people to account when needed and can be tough. Especially the latter is, perhaps unexpectedly, relatively often found to be a skill that is lacking in leaders. Leaders often want to be liked.

6) Well-performing leaders tend to possess sound judgement, trustworthiness and have integrity. There is a significant correlation between intelligence and success in leadership, but the former is not a guarantee for the latter. In other words, for leaders, some intelligence may be enough. Clearly, the other characteristics mentioned here play a role, too.

7) A profound characteristic of successful leaders is that they tend to have a vision. Perhaps this comes closest to what we think of when we consider what the activity of leading is essentially about. Leaders shows the direction of travel; they have their sights set on a destination. Leaders with a vision have a compelling story that persuades staff to work for the collective good and wins support from wider stakeholders. Strong leaders paint a picture, inspire their followers and thus shape the behaviour and aspirational trajectory of

their organisation. These leaders set a strategy, or they are on a mission.

8) Perhaps before all other nine characteristics listed here, and thus pointing to a developmental dynamic (i.e. much of leadership can be learnt), is the notion that successful leaders have a good dose of self-awareness. Perhaps more important than all of the above aspects, this is a starting point for leaders to direct themselves, and grow and develop. People with inflated views or denial of their weaknesses will be less able to build a full leadership team in which leaders complement one another.

Good leaders cannot be good at everything; strong leadership exists by virtue of a strong team of leaders that complement one another within the senior leadership team. Self-awareness is key in that. Some leaders naturally excel in strategy, some in people management and relationship building, and some in, for instance, operational delivery. Moreover, good leaders exist by the virtue of those that are led by them; their followers. In the future, it is likely that these roles may be more interchangeable, transient and less well-defined. Ambiguous, agile roles, in line with the agile and fluid nature of the work being done.

9) Leaders that perform well regularly ask for critical feedback; weaker leaders, in fact, do the opposite and ask for such feedback far less often. The advice then is for aspiring leaders to be courageous and determined to learn from the ugly, if seemingly subjective, truth, where the feedback is a tool towards incremental learning and self-development.

10) As a last point, the advice from a psychological perspective is to not just embrace the future, but to embrace one's self, in order to make a meaningful and somehow still selfless contribution to that future.

Psychologically future-proof leaders

To function successfully in the future, leaders will need to be open to the unknown changes that this future will bring. Psychological factors play a huge role in this; technology not only relies on people to be developed, but also to be adopted by people. The mindset and personalities of leaders will influence how they behave and how effective they are. This, in turn, will play an even greater role in shaping the wellbeing and productivity of the people they lead – and themselves.

About the author

Jan P. de Jonge MA AFBPsS PPABP

www.peoplebusinesspsychology.com

Jan is a business psychologist whose consultancy People Business Psychology Ltd. ® (est. 2012) works internationally with clients from all industries, applying research-based approaches in psychology to develop excellence in leaders and professionals, capitalizing on personality, entrepreneurial potential, leadership style, ability and emotional intelligence.

The Role of Feedback in Managing Performance

By Marjory Mair

'O wad some Power the giftie gie us, to see oursels as ithers see us!'

(Trans.: Oh would some Power the gift give us, to see ourselves as others see us.)

Robert Burns, Scottish Poet

Introduction

He said, "You should speak up more in these meetings". "Really?" I questioned with great surprise. "You're a great listener. Thank you so much for this morning". I smiled, shook hands and left floating out the building – in my book, that was the greatest compliment and my self-esteem bucket is full to the brim. "I'm asking you because I know you'll tell me what you really think". I smile and say "okay" and inwardly hope that this is not going to be too difficult.

In the chapter by Heather Mills, she outlines many of the drivers for change in the workplace. We all know it is becoming increasingly complex and challenging whether we work in the public, private or not-for-profit sectors. Success in the future means engaging the workforce, building teams, empowering individuals and creating innovative working environments. Gone are the days of command and control leadership where people just do what they are told to do. Setting direction with clear goals and working with an agreed set of values and behaviours means our people have more autonomy to work and to make timely decisions within defined boundaries. However, with the clearest of objectives and the best of intentions, things don't go quite according to plan and that's where feedback enters the scene.

Without feedback, individuals and teams unwittingly carry-on with mediocre or poor performance, often oblivious when everyone else is aware – it becomes the conversation in the kitchens, canteens and the corridors, the coffee shops, the cubby-holes, the conference rooms and even in the carparks. Unfortunately, the conversation often involves everyone except the person or the people who can do something about it – whatever 'it' may be.

So, going forward, the ability to have an open, honest conversation, a dialogue, not a dumping session, where feedback is given and received in a considered and respectful way is not a nice to have but a need to have skill of Business Leaders for the future.

Funnily enough as I reflect on my experience of receiving feedback it's the encouraging stuff that immediately springs to mind and then as I begin to recall other occasions when the feedback wasn't just encouraging but also helpful "I thought it was an engaging start to the presentation although I didn't get the link to the topic?" "Your stories are great, but I think they need to be a bit shorter".

And then of course there are the times when feedback I've received has been seriously bad! Vague, given in a large group, critical with opinion and no facts or no credibility from the person giving it. Fortunately, over the years, whipping on my imaginary non-stick coat, when I see that stuff coming, protects me, and the giver of the feedback might as well spit in the wind! More recently however, I catch it in my imaginary colander and take out anything that might be helpful or worth exploring and when I'm in the right mindset i.e. the anger or the shock has dissipated, I'll find the time (face to face if possible) to say thank you, explore it more and then take the opportunity to give feedback.

Often though, when corrective feedback is given, it's not the actual message that is the problem but more the way it is given e.g. if someone's lateness is causing issues they need to know, but they don't need sarcastic comments like 'big fight with the duvet this morning?' or threats "if you don't get here on time tomorrow …." or commands "don't be late again".

Here's my biggest tip about feedback - make it a habit and catch them doing it right. When you see people doing something good, well or over and above, take a moment to appreciate it and get some deposits in what Stephen Covey calls the Relationship Bank Account, Covey, Steven R, *Seven Habits of Highly Effective People* (1999), Simon and Schuster, and then when there are issues that need addressing it's not such a big deal – you've made some strong deposits, so when you're at risk of making a withdrawal, it doesn't empty the account or put you in the red.

'A five-to-one ratio of appreciation to criticism

helps people think for themselves.

'Change takes place best in a large context of genuine praise'

Kline, Nancy, *Time to Think,* (1999), Ward Lock.

It saddens me when I hear people tell me "the only time my manager speaks to me is when I've done something wrong" or just the other day I heard "you can do 99.9% of your job well, nothing is said and 0.01% goes wrong and they come down on you like a ton of bricks".

What is feedback?

It's a **conversation** where you **share your observations** in a **constructive** way and open a **dialogue** to **create clarity** and encourage **better performance**.

> *'Feedback should provide value for the receiver*
> *not a release for the giver.'*
>
> *Anon*

Why is it important?

- It builds trust
- It's the only way to close the gap between poor and good or good and great performance
- If done badly or not at all, it damages relationships and limits potential and performance in the long term.

There are two aspects of feedback that will help make you a great Leader...

1. Giving Feedback
2. Receiving Feedback

1. Giving Feedback

Signs of doing it badly
- Launching into it without any preparation
- Doing it when you are annoyed or frustrated
- Sharing your opinion rather than factual evidence
- Focusing on being right, looking good and winning!
- Giving it to everyone when it's only relevant to one or a few
- Talking to others about it rather than the person who needs to hear it

How do I do it well?

- Be clear on the why you are giving feedback and what you want to achieve
- Make it factually based (do your homework)
- Create the right environment for the discussion – somewhere private
- See models below for more ways to prepare, structure and deliver your feedback.

Top 10 Tips for Giving Feedback

1. Catch them 'doing it right', and fill up the relationship bank account so that they are open to a conversation when things haven't gone so well

2. Start with a belief that whatever the person/s did, they had a positive intention; they didn't get out of bed that morning determined to make mistakes and upset you.

3. Give yourself some feedback first and ask "what is my intention in starting this conversation"?

4. Make it face to face wherever possible – don't chicken out and send an email – yes it might be easier but easier for who and whose performance is this about? Okay, okay, good point - ultimately yours so you need to do this well.

5. Gather the facts e.g. how late on what days and what exactly was unprofessional about the situation – what did you hear and see e.g. rather than "that was very unprofessional", say "when you tutted, rolled your eyes and walked off without replying, I found that very rude and unprofessional".

6. Take time to prepare the feedback when possible.

7. Take ownership of your thoughts and feelings by using 'I statements' rather than 'you statements' e.g. "I don't agree with that", rather than "You're wrong".

8. Avoid coming up with The Solution to allow the other person to take ownership.

9. Don't share the feedback with everyone when it related to only one or a few. In other words, the team meeting is not the place when it doesn't relate to the whole team.

10. Breathe, pause and don't be afraid of silence when delivering the feedback. You get 7 seconds before it becomes awkward.

2. Receiving Feedback

Signs of doing it badly
- Assuming you don't need it and never ask for it
- Assuming you understand it when you don't
- When you do receive feedback, justifying it or explaining it e.g. it's okay for me because …
- Ignoring it when you do get it
- Brushing it away e.g. if it's a complement, refuse it; if it's corrective, refuse it

How do I do it well?
- Stop what you are doing and listen.
- 'Seek first to understand, then be understood' is a phrase from Seven Habits of Highly Effective People (Covey, Steven R, Simon and Schuster 1999). If you don't understand and need more information, ask for it e.g. when did I do that, or what exactly was

it that I said … or "what would you have preferred on that occasion?"

- Say thank you! If it's from a team member, it's likely to have taken them a lot of courage to say what they, and often others, are thinking. So "thank you for taking the time to raise this issue…"
- See that it can be a gift – even if you just keep the wrapping or part of the message.
- You have a choice about what you do with the feedback – it's like chocolate cake!

Photo by Food Photographer | Jennifer Pallian on Unsplash

	Chocolate Cake	Feedback
Option One	Say thank you and eat it immediately because it looks delicious and you want it.	Say thank you and take it on board immediately because it is well presented and helpful.
Option Two	Say thank you and put it in the fridge for a more suitable time later.	Say thank you and you'll think about it and look into it more (maybe ask for more details).
Option Three	Go and look at it in the fridge later and eat the icing and put the rest in the bin because you just like the icing.	Have a think about it and decide some of it helpful so take that on board and ignore the rest.
Option Four	Say thank you and put it in the bin or offer it to someone else	Say thank you and ignore it.

On the basis that feedback can be a gift, whatever you do, say "thank you" for something otherwise you head for the trap of living the Andy Stanley quote: "leaders who don't listen, will eventually be surrounded by people who have nothing to say".

Helpful Models

Here are five practical models that will help you prepare, give and evaluate feedback.

1. Mind the Gap Model

The Gap Model, created with one of my Associates, Christine Garner, is helpful in preparing to give feedback. And just like getting over any gap, it needs a **STEP** so:

Set the scene – 1:1, in private, allow uninterrupted time

Tell the facts clearly – the expected standard or the policy against the actual standard or behaviour

Explore the reason for the gap – listen, ask questions to understand more, resist making assumptions and jumping to conclusions.

Plan the action to close the gap – encourage the other person to identify the solutions before offering your own views and set a date to review progress and provide additional support if necessary.

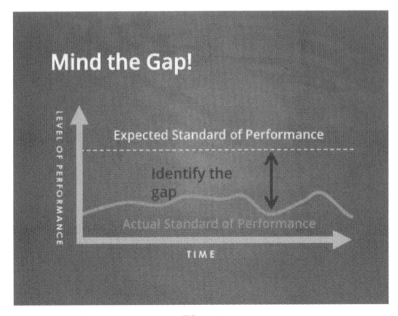

2. The DESC Model

- **Describe** the behaviour e.g. when you turn up late for meetings
- **Express** your concerns about the situation e.g. it seems as if it's not that important to you and then we need to spend time bringing you up to speed
- **Suggest** alternative or **State** what needs to happen e.g. so how can you get to the meetings on time?
- **Consequences** – both positive and negative e.g. because your colleagues are getting hacked off and I do know you have got a lot of useful input at the meeting if we can start it on the right note.

3. The UHT Model

Here's a handy little template from Annie Clarke of Annie's Training Company for crafting your feedback. You can pull it out in the moment once you've practised it a couple of times.

I **U**nderstand ..... **H**owever .... **T**herefore ....

E.g. I <u>understand</u> you've got a lot on at the moment <u>however</u> our deadline for X is tomorrow <u>therefore</u> I need you to work on that as the priority today.

4. Smart Questions

If you need more information, use Open Questions. Rudyard Kipling's poem helps us along:

> "I had six honest serving men,
>
> They taught me all I knew,
>
> Their names are what and why and when
>
> And how and where and who."

Open questions act as the key to information, greater understanding, the act of co-creation and empowerment and ultimately better decisions.

5. Time for TED

If you still don't have enough input or understanding from the other person on either the cause of the gap in performance or behaviour and your open questions are running out, bring in TED

Like any skill, the ability to give and receive feedback comes with practice.

Enjoy the journey and any feedback on this chapter will be very welcome – I promise I won't explain, justify or make excuses however I might ask a few questions.

About the Author

Marjory Mair

https://mmairassociates.com

Marjory Mair Associates exist to see leaders leading high performing teams and influencing their organisations for good. We believe that organisations are about people so we work alongside company CEO's and senior teams, to develop existing leaders and foster new talent in order to stimulate growth and performance. We create environments where leaders are trusted and affirmed and are set free to think creatively and act courageously. We are passionate about 'values-based' leadership and our approach is to affirm and encourage leaders, to develop sustainable solutions.

With over 20 years' experience working in across all sectors Marjory is known for being approachable but assertive, professional but engaging and enjoys working collaboratively with leaders to navigate complex issues.

Developing Teams for the Future – is it still relevant?

By Adrian Wheatley

As organisations change and develop to meet current and new challenges, so must the individuals they employ. Much time, energy and money is often invested in developing the skills of individuals but what about team development? In business, people are often structured in teams according to the organisation chart but how many teams take a conscious approach to making sure that the team is performing effectively as a unit?

Continuing advances in technology and more and more demand for remote and flexible working mean that teams are now less and less likely to be located together all of the time. This reduces personal contact and so requires even more effort to ensure that the team functions well and continues to develop.

Workforce composition is also changing; Millennials are likely to want more informal working relationships with less reliance on hierarchy, 'Baby Boomers' are working beyond retirement age, diversity and inclusion of cultures and nationalities is increasing.

With all of these changes, team development seems even less likely to happen organically than it is now.

This chapter outlines two established models describing team performance followed by a real example illustrating how team development can work in practice. There is also a quick diagnostic tool to help you to decide where and how you might invest in team development activity.

Assessing Where the Team is Today

Bruce Tuckman's (1965) well known 'Forming-Storming-Norming-Performing' model outlines the stages teams go through as they develop towards maturity. He believed that teams can move through the stages by taking specific actions and are likely to find themselves 'stuck', remaining immature and less effective, unless they do so. Teams can often regress to earlier stages as team members move on and are replaced by new ones.

Katzenbach & Smith research ('The Wisdom of Teams' 2015) suggested that in order for a team to deliver collective work, performance results and personal growth they should focus on building the commitment, skills and accountability of the individuals in the team.

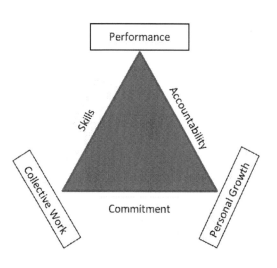

Understanding the current effectiveness of the team normally starts with the leader supplying an outline of the team, its history and the answers to a number of key questions such as;

- What are the team leader's aspirations for the team
- Where is the team currently on Tuckman's continuum?

- How does the team perform when compared to the Katzenbach & Smith model?

After this, it is often worthwhile getting the wider team's view. This can be done either by using a simple diagnostic questionnaire or by face-to-face discussions (or over the telephone) depending on geography and level of investment.

Deciding What to Do To Improve Performance

There is no 'one-size-fits-all' way to develop a team. Much will depend on what the team is trying to achieve and where it is starting from as defined by the diagnostic phase above.

1. Future teams, possibly thrown together by an organisational restructure, may require support to help them from 'forming' to 'storming'. Here the initial focus could simply be on techniques to accelerate team members in getting to know each other and developing a deeper understanding of their individual responsibilities as described by the new job descriptions.

2. In another scenario, teams are usually impacted by the appointment of a new leader and this can be especially difficult if the team leader is being promoted to manage a team of former peers. It may be that supporting the team leader through coaching to help them consider the desired state of the team is all that is needed initially.

3. A team may be charged with improving its overall performance as business pressure or competition increase. This may require the team to re-assess the team's purpose, what success looks like and which skills and ways of working they will need to develop (or drop) to raise its game.

It may be that all three of the above scenarios happen at the same time and so this may require a more comprehensive plan supported by individual as well as team interventions.

All of the above can be particularly challenging where the new team is based in different sites or even countries. It is also likely that different generations of workers will have different expectations of how they can benefit from teamwork.

In any event, before investing time and money into team development, it is best to have a clear statement of the desired outcomes and the return on investment that is expected. This will make evaluation of the team development easier.

Case Study – A real team example

 *This was a senior team who led a growing division within a privately-owned group. The business operated across two sites, 200 miles apart and with senior team members based at both sites. There was also a matrix structure with some team members having 'dotted line' functional responsibilities to the wider group but each member reported directly to the team leader. The leader had been appointed from outside the business and had the experience of managing larger, more complex operations. The team was a mix of gender, age and experience.*

Diagnostic – where are we today?

The team leader's view was that his appointment, followed by a re-structure of the team meant that it was firmly in the 'forming' phase according to Tuckman's model. Although some most of the team had been in the previous iteration of the team, there was enough change for it to essentially be seen as a new team.

The individuals in the team were interviewed and their views summarised as follows:

Team Element	Team Member and Team Leader Views
Common Purpose	*The team mostly thought that the team's purpose was clear but didn't think the team talked about it in the same way.* *The team leader thought that the purpose was not clear within the team and that it was not aligned to business priorities.*
Performance Goals	*Team members thought that they set challenging individual goals and that team goal priorities were clear.* *The team leader agreed that team members had challenging individual goals but that team goals were neither clear nor understood.*
Working Approach	*Team members thought that communication within the team was frequent but that discussions within the team were not open and honest and feedback to improve performance in the team was absent.* *The team leader largely agreed with the team members' comments although he did think that feedback to improve performance was present.*

Mutual Accountability	*Team members thought they understood what each member's personal and joint responsibilities were but that team members did not take responsibility for the performance of the team.*
	The team leader disagreed that responsibilities were understood within the team. He also thought that the team did not measure itself against team goals.
Complementary Skills	*Although willing to spend time supporting each other, the team members did not think that the team had all of the skills that it required to be effective. They also didn't see opportunities for growth in their current roles.*
	The team leader mostly agreed with the team but did not see them as supportive of each other.

Design – how do we approach this?

Based on the above, and in the context of the team leader's view that the team was in the 'storming' phase of development, it was decided to involve the team in two workshops a few months apart with these desired outcomes:

- *Deeper, more trusting relationships within the team*

- *Agreement on a number of key ways of working improvements*

- *Key priorities and success factors outlined for the next 12 months*

- *Enhanced buy-in and support of the team members*

Delivery – engaging with the team

Early on in workshop 1 the results of the diagnostic were played back to the team to provoke discussion, to check understanding and to inform any design changes to be made during the event or where the level of discussion in the team meant there may be areas requiring special focus.

The discussion was lively and revealed to the team a number of key issues:

1. *The team members thought that the purpose of the team was 'strategy' whereas in the context of the wider group their focus was clearly 'delivery'.*
2. *There was no common understanding of collective accountability for meeting team goals.*
3. *While team members respected each other, their ways of working in respect to meetings and decision making were poor.*

These realisations helped to focus the team on making best use of the workshop time and committing to a joint action plan for improvement. The team leader took the opportunity to outline his vision for the Division and how it fitted with the wider Group's strategy. At the end of the second workshop the team presented their action plans to a senior representative of the Group who was then able to feedback to the team.

Evaluation – was it worth it?

Each member of the team was asked to complete an evaluation after the workshops which suggested that they were all satisfied that the desired outcomes were met.

The feedback from the Group visitor was very positive in that he could see a visible commitment to both the 'what' and the 'how' of the team's objectives.

The team's action plan provided a structure and explicit actions to improving the performance of the team. Progress against the plan was reviewed at each subsequent team meeting and specific responsibilities included in personal objectives.

The team leader had secured clear commitment to the purpose of the team and an agreed action plan to measure personal and mutual accountability to team performance. The team had moved from the 'forming' stage through 'storming' at the workshops and ultimately started to 'norm' how the team worked together.

So what does this all mean?

The team in the above case study was diverse geographically, by gender and experience. Future teams are likely to be even more diverse in their makeup and with a wider range of expectations from team members.

It seems, then, that focus on team development will require more focus rather than less in our ever-more-complex world. There is no 'one way' to develop a team; so much depends on where the team is starting from, what it is trying to achieve and the current and future ability of the team members.

Are you ready to invest?

To make sure that time and energy is not wasted it is critical to carry out a diagnostic which gives a clear picture of where the team is starting from.

The following questions may help you to decide to what extent you need to invest and the level of support you may need.

- What is the vision for your team in the future? (say, 6-12 months from now)
- How would you describe your team today in terms of its collective performance?
- What challenges is the team facing both now and in the future?
- What are the key drivers for investing in team development at this time?
- How will you measure the return on investment in team development?
- If you do decide to invest the time and energy in creating a high performing team who will be responsible for leading the activity?
- Would the team development activity benefit from external support?

About the author

Adrian Wheatley

www.adrianwheatley.co.uk

Adrian's experience comes from a career spent in Human Resources and Learning & Development roles across a variety of industry sectors and organisations, both large and small: FMCG, Legal, Defence/Aerospace and Financial Services. He has held UK, European and Global roles and through these he has worked with senior leaders as HR manager/business partner, coach and facilitator in strategic, operational and international contexts.

He is a Member of the Chartered Institute of Personnel and Development, holds an MA in Human Resource Management and a Diploma in Management Coaching & Mentoring

Adrian likes to divide his social time between sailing and spending time in Spain where he has family.

Pushing the boundaries to ensure success!

By Samantha Pennell

Summary Points

There are many operational and strategic factors to consider in ensuring ongoing success as our workforce evolves. This chapter explores some of those key factors and considerations for leaders in increasing the effectiveness of the role and therefore ensuring the future success of business through becoming more flexible.

The key takeaways will be:

- Exploration of where increasingly flexible approaches are needed in job role, working time, location of work, benefits, embracing technology, workforce planning, learning and development and hierarchy.
- Suggestions on how to increase flexibility in these areas and enable ongoing business success in the future.

Introduction

Times have changed so rapidly in the last century. With the evolution of modern technology, it has arguably been the biggest cultural shift in the history of humans. 100 years ago, our world was, for the most part, our immediate vicinity; our street and our local area with deliveries of milk and coal being made to our houses set up through local business orders.

(My road in the Victorian era!)

Fast forward and we find ourselves with a constant and real-time global outlook on life built around speed and convenience. We are usually connected to a device at any point in time and quite often more than one. We have the capability to video call someone on the other side of the world and ask a conversational AI bot to boil the kettle for a cup of tea at the same time as we can check how well we slept last night on our smart watch.

When we talk about our past organisations, we might hear reference to 'a job for life' and a structured approach as to how we got things done – increasing efficiency by doing the same thing faster. Innovation could have been a function within a business or sometimes a one-off special initiative rather than part of every person's daily work life. Now we have a complex mix of generations and cultures in our businesses so need to be adaptable to different views, priorities and outlooks.

So, what do we need to consider? With all these distractions from our connected devices, it can be hard to pay attention to ensuring successful leadership.

Flexibility is the answer

There is an evolving shift in thought for workers to 'what does this mean for me?' Value-added contribution is gained from the flexibility to innovate, collaborate and develop. The advantage this can bring to a leader is to ensure a diverse and empowered organisation that is always driving success and innovation – who could ask for more?!

Flexibility is the key to the success of any organisation of the future and this can be divided in to subsets aligned to ways of working which are listed below. Each has an explanation as to how it is evolving and questions to ask when looking at how increasing flexibility can maximise return on investment and ensure continued success:

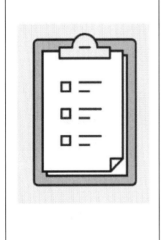

Job role

A Principal Statement of employment must contain a job title and a brief job description. This is to enable an agreed alignment of expectation of delivery but with changing views of business contribution and the accelerated natural evolution of roles to align with technological changes, could this be a potential challenge?

Should leaders review roles themselves to ascertain whether they can be more flexible? Can leaders enable workers to move to multiple roles and extend approaches to roles within businesses, for example, with job rotation or project placement; external partners, collaboration and dual function roles?

Working time

A Principal Statement of employment must contain hours worked. Traditionally this has also included what those hours are. Should we look at a more flexible approach and focus on achievement over clock-watching?

For generations coming in to the workplace, there is a shift to an increasing desire to establish individual business ventures, be it combining employment with freelancing or to set up boutique businesses, often aligned to social consciousness e.g. someone setting up an online business selling Vegan clothes whilst working as a Consultant in IT. There is the traditional requirement for flexing around childcare and with our ageing population, some people are opting for reducing working hours to enable care for elderly parents and relatives so coming full circle.

Location of work

Again, this should be included in the Principal Statement, but can we test this and use terms like 'virtual' and increase flexibility around where the job is done?

The amount of space occupied by workers has decreased over the years and with the increase in networking and businesses embracing the use of social media and best practice sharing, many roles can be location independent.

One thing to bear in mind is the importance of delivery with social interaction – there needs to be a common footprint. How best can we establish the team formation and work through the traditional and successful approach of team formation – forming-storming-norming-performing? To get this working at its best, there could be an argument that the strongest start point is to bring the team together to work through the formation stage, build trust and then enable virtual working from there – we are pack animals after all!!

Benefits

Of course, the more traditional benefits such as a pension scheme are still important – don't we all plan to live our lives after work in the Maldives?! We can but dream! With workers expecting to be more mobile and move from business to business when the opportunity arises, we need to look at this from a wider perspective and be innovative and flexible in our approach to benefit provision.

What do leaders offer that is not money driven? For example, do we demonstrate consideration for wellbeing, volunteering and social consciousness? Businesses that focus on environmental factors are more attractive. Volunteer days and green days are considered great perks and also present the opportunity for positive marketing in the local community.

Stress and mental health are now much more talked about subjects than we've ever experienced before and with the constant availability of information it is really important individuals take care with the reassuring support of leaders.

Embracing technology

This is a relentless requirement as technology is constantly evolving and we need to have a flexible, positive, and pro-active approach as innovations transition to become a part of every-day life.

There is an amusing story told of a child who swiped a photo in a newspaper to see the next one. Everyone laughed but is that really so far away? Harry Potter suggests not!

We can review how we can be more engaging and interactive in our communication with technology for example, a leader may send out a regular email newsletter to update workers on business news. How about moving to an interactive blog where people can take part too? It is a brave move and there will be some people who may defy logic with their responses but in general people want to generate great ideas and drive businesses forward.

There is an increase in the use of collaboration tools that allow ongoing communications, updates, file sharing and team collaboration in one application moving away from the requirement for many different applications to maximise interactions.

When a leader is looking to promote a business to bring new talent in to the organisation, the points of touch online are now limitless and are becoming more and more integrated with AI and machine learning to streamline selection without bias (although as is our nature, we often try to find ways to circumnavigate this to ensure criteria are met such as researching key words against roles!). This means the traditional approach of using agencies or executive search businesses is changing although they do still play their part depending on the context of the requirement.

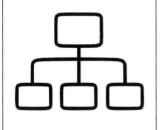

Workforce planning

The traditional approach is to work top down by defining the profit required from a product or service then to review the number of people required to sell the required amount versus the cost of delivery.

Adopting a more flexible and strategic, albeit longer-term option is to forecast the ambition of the business, understand what talent is needed in the medium term and target universities to create good connections and networks to recruit from and grow in to the business. From there and building a bottom-up picture, a review can be made of cost, budget, and resource.

Learning and development

For new joiners to a business, an increased number of individuals are seeking open communication and support with guidance at first but then the freedom to make their role their own with ongoing support as needed.

Traditionally people who have achieved in their current role are often primed for promotion in to leadership roles which require soft skills and leadership they may not have previously acquired.

Can we enable this through a more flexible approach to learning using situational leadership rather than traditional classroom or virtual learning? For example, taking real-time examples of issues to a group of new leaders and asking them to work collaboratively to define solutions and approaches; introducing skilled worker forums and mentor programmes.

For those working on projects, we could take it one step further than having a lessons-learnt session post-delivery and work with a new team just about to

	embark on a project. This would not only generate new ideas and protect the future project but support networking and sponsorship. The same could be done for people moving in to and out of specific roles.
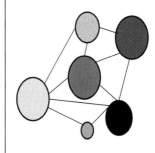	**Hierarchy** How flexible are our leaders when it comes to re-arranging the career and succession planning ladders?! A controversial question could be do we need functional managers? If an approach to business is flexible and agile with workers fulfilling multiple roles, does the functional and operational part of the leadership role become defunct and what then for the future? Rather than closing this book now and walking away, let us look at a flexible approach to this – what about having leaders with a different approach? It may not be about being the power person who decides the promotion/salary/performance but a mentor or sponsor to collaborate and enable the development and support of the individual. We can all think of a great leader and a poor one and would say the great one is an inspiration. This moves away from the rather stuffy Teddy Roosevelt's approach of 'Strenuous Life' by working all available

	hours regardless of work-life balance with no mention of actually achieving success but aspiring to move to Sheryl Sandberg's world of leadership to 'make others better as a result of your presence and making sure that impact lasts in your absence.'
	'After all, the function of leadership is to produce more leaders not more followers' – Ralph Nader.

The vision – five years from now....

It is an unfortunate inevitability we will all have more wrinkles... unless one of the new innovations from changing how we work leads to an amazing solution to that for all of us!

There is quite a lot for leaders to think about and prepare for looking in to the future as their role evolves. In 5 years' time, a leader's role will be even more about inspiration and vision and less about the metrics of running and organisation. This would need to be managed by another specialist role in the organisation focussing on mechanics and governance. There will need to be a clear strategy regarding skills requirements so we can grow our talent from the bottom up. For example, what do we need now to grow AI within a business in the next 5 years? We will need to review this strategy on a regular and ongoing basis as it will be a continuous cycle and we will need to farm the talent from education establishments.

What can we do to be more flexible in our approach? It is important to have a strategic approach to the future both from a technical and people point of view.

What is important to consider? Top tips

Provided below are some take-aways where increasingly flexible approaches will enable success:

- **Job Role:** Leaders will need to consider careful and effective resource management and initiatives to organically grow with learning and development opportunities, for example with job rotation.
- **Working Time:** Workers are moving to flexible hours aligned to their own lifestyle including being able to focus on areas of passion such as family time, boutique businesses and social projects and also to align to the requirement of roles as global interactions across different time zones increase.
- **Location of Work**: With the increase of flexible hours and agile working, the idea of an office space will not be necessary. Workers will not need to travel to the same office every day so building budgets could be invested in other areas. It is recommended, however, there is still a physical collaboration space to enable team relationships to form and have ongoing and continuous check-in, meet up and case study learning opportunities when required.......Although, who knows in five to ten years' time maybe we can holograph ourselves into meetings and conversations and physical gatherings won't be necessary at all!!
- **Benefits:** Leaders will need to ensure the company grows and extends its wellbeing philosophy and corporate social responsibility ethics to incorporate the needs and drivers of its workforce. This can be used as a key attraction tool.
- **Embracing Technology:** Leaders need to extend points of touch online to maximise market and internal reach and look to implementing collaboration tools that enable interactions to happen in one place rather than across numerous applications.

- **Workforce Planning:** Leaders need to drive this from the bottom up rather than from profit generation down to enable continuous growth.
- **Learning & Development:** Leaders can look to drive more of the 70-20-10 learning model rather than employing traditional push learning techniques. This can be done through using real-time learning workshops with those who have experienced the challenge and then mentor those new to it.
- **Hierarchy:** Teams will be constantly evolving and dissolving and as successful leaders, we will need to include as part of our remit, a mentor focussed approach in collaboration with wider teams, collation of feedback and an ongoing check on the wellbeing of workers.

Promoting flexibility within a business may not be a massive financial change but will certainly elicit a cultural shift – as Trevor Ragan says in his Ted Talks YouTube episode – do you want to be a 'jungle tiger or a zoo tiger?!' – do we want to be fed by someone else and maintain the status quo or be challenged, take risk and grow?

Learn how to get out of your comfort zone to push the boundaries and ensure success!

About the author

Samantha Pennell

Samantha Pennell is a CIPD qualified HR professional with 25 years' experience. She has fulfilled generalist roles across manufacturing, IT, telecommunications and professional services industry sectors. She has led specialist projects in change management, employee relations, training and development and sales strategy. She has worked for all sizes of business from start-ups to large corporations in freelance, fixed term and permanent roles. Samantha lives in Ascot, Berkshire and enjoys trying new things out of the ordinary such as fire-breathing!

Leadership – Why Technology will make Leaders more Human

By Siân Perham

As the world becomes more technologically driven, so the greater the challenge becomes for leaders to inspire, engage and excite others to high performance and to deliver exceptional business results.

Two thirds of the worlds' population have a mobile device in 2019 (Statista.com). For workplaces, the upside this global connection and collaboration has resulted in teams boosting productivity, increasing efficiency and inspiring creativity. The downside of technology has resulted in human interaction that has become more transactional and functional.

Never has there been a time for leadership development to be so high on the business agenda. Never has there been more fluidity of where people work, how they work, when they work, the age they work, their expectations of work. Businesses will depend on the quality of their leadership more than ever before to meet the challenges of the future work environment.

In this chapter you will learn;

- How leaders of the future will need to be different to today
- Four building blocks to transform leadership capability fit for the future
- Hints and tips for a practical approach to start building leadership capability from today.

Research by Virgin on the future of work, identifies 5 key people themes relating to the future for work;

- People want to work for organisations with purpose
- People will expect lifelong growth
- Leaders will need to help manage the '24/7' culture created by technology
- Leaders with the skills to connect people and ideas will be in demand
- The concept of work will be one of mutual benefit and making a difference.

Gone is the need for leaders who know it all, have all the answers, technical skill and who tell others what to do. Leaders in the future will have the 'human' factor. Which is to say they will have the skills, behaviours and mindset to; realise the talent of others, attract people and their energy towards achieving a vision. All whilst creating an individual experience that is personalised, holistic, rewarding, purposeful, valuable, developmental and allows individuals to make a difference in a way that works for them – wherever in the world they may be.

What is identified is a huge skills gap between leaders today and leaders of tomorrow. Leaders today are often promoted to leadership positions off the back of an excellent reputation built on a technical skill or expertise. The result is organisations filled with leaders who are doing their best with what they've got. Which quite honestly, is not good enough.

In the current climate, leadership is a really tough job, and is set to become ever more challenging. It will require a leap beyond intellectual capability and just 'doing' people processes. It requires leaders who bring the human factor; the ability to create an experience that is personalised, holistic, rewarding, creates purpose, valuable, developmental and allows individuals opportunity to make a difference and one where individuals would choose to invest.

In summary, the leaders with the human factor;

- are connectors of people and ideas
- leverage technology to influence, motivate, engage, excite and inspire
- are agile and flexible
- attract and develop talented individuals to invest their time, energy and effort in your business
- build work environments that deliver great results.

So, what does this mean for Leadership Development and what can businesses to do get their leaders ready for the future?

TIPS

- Start by treating leaders as you want and need them to behave in the future
- Identify and nurture the leaders in your business who demonstrate a willingness to learn, and an ability to learn from experience, NOT technical competence.

With such a transformation of leadership on the horizon, leadership development should be looking to close the gap on leadership skills, as they have never been more critical. The need is to build a next generation of leaders who will communicate better, think more creatively, strategically, be more collaborative, be more empathetic and much more.

The question is how to start or build on your current leadership development program. Outlined below is the Aligned Leadership Framework to future proof your leadership capability.

The Leader

Self Awareness - Great leadership starts with the individual.

Inspiring Leadership in the future will start and end with the individual and their own behaviour. Successful leadership will require authenticity, emotional intelligence, learning agility, strategic thinking, honesty, curiosity, courage and integrity. Leaders will need to understand who they are, what drives their behaviour, and be the leader their teams need them to be.

Human evolution will need to speed up to have any chance of keeping up with the pace of change in the external world. Neuroscience will have a much greater importance in leadership and understanding how the brain controls both mindset and behaviour. For individuals to be authentic leaders, they will need to know and understand themselves at a level beyond what is expected today. Leaders will need to create time and space to understand the inner workings of their own minds - build an awareness of their own inner dialogue, explore their mindset, identify their enablers and barriers, know their strengths and weaknesses, their limitations, their values and their boundaries.

Self-awareness lays the foundation for great leadership. The significance of the mindset shift required of leaders in the future is one of the most significant seen in recent history and creating learning environments that support leaders to explore and build their self-awareness will build a strong foundation and accelerate their leadership success.

TIPS

- Support leaders in their personal development
- Create opportunity for your leaders to become the leaders they aspire to be
- Invest in your leaders personal development, as they are investing a lot of their time, effort and energy

Environments that excite

Creating work environments in which people choose to invest and give their greatest performance.

We all have more choice now than ever before when it comes to our careers and so one of the greatest leadership challenges will be to create environments where people will choose to invest their time, energy and give their best performance to your business whilst fulfilling their own purpose, goals and objectives. Work will become more of a reciprocal relationship more than ever before.

Leaders who achieve great things need to set positive intention and understand that people come first. Exciting environments in the future will rely on leaders who foster three elements;

> **Trust** – work will increasingly become about human connection and so future leaders will need to know the importance of both trusting and be trusted. To trust and be trusted is what underpins every relationship. In a working

world that is becoming smaller, flatter, agile, faster paced, and virtual, the key success factor will be trust.

Trust is simply not just 'something' that a leader does. It is about that human factor and the intent that leaders set. A leaders' capability to build trust will enable others to feel comfortable to share; ideas, thoughts and opinions, it boosts motivation, and increases productivity and collaboration resulting in better business outcomes and happier customers.

Empowerment – the transformation of leadership away from technical skill and competence to empowering others will require individuals to take responsibility and accountability.

Success will be created through a leader's ability to harness energy, enthusiasm and action around vision and purpose, and enabling teams to define their path to success whilst being there to support and challenge along the way.

Environments that excite will be built by outcome driven leadership, trust and empowerment. Creating environments where people can make a difference, have purpose, learn, grow, take a risk, and develop.

Resilience – In the future, one certainty is that the world will become more complex which places greater demands on people, and great leadership will rely on the 'human factor' and recognizing the whole 'human being' to enable individuals to juggle many balls, of which work will be just one. Environments that excite will build and support an individual's personal resilience. Enabling individuals to manage their energy; physically, emotionally, mentally and socially, will positively impact wellbeing, energy and engagement levels.

TIPS

- Leaders will require the right skills, mindset and behaviours to enable their leadership transformation
- Three key skills to develop as part of the leadership culture;
  - Great Listening
  - Powerful Coaching
  - Honest Communication

The Team – From Task to People Focus

Leadership fit for the future requires a fundamental shift from management by performance and competence to outcome focused leadership. Delivering exceptional business results through identifying the best talent, developing talent and focusing on the 'whole' person.

Leaders will need the 'super' human factor to address one of the greatest leadership challenges facing leaders in the future; to be genuinely curious about the people around them which requires a fundamental shift away from the job/task and making assumptions about others to observe and be curious about those people around them. By that, leaders of the future will need to look beyond the 'what' it is their teams do and focus on the 'whole' human being.

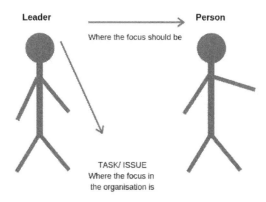

Leaders will need to acknowledge and understand that people don't all see the world in the same way. Every individual has a different story; background, experiences and way of seeing the world. The success factor for great leadership will be a leader who can flex and adapt to the situation and the person in order to offer what it is the other person wants and needs.

In a world where leadership is no longer reliant on leaders knowing the answers and telling people what to do, the ability to communicate effectively will be paramount. Creating environments where people feel comfortable to have open and honest dialogue about what is going on for them, to discuss performance, development, feedback, and share personal information, will test the boundaries and their thoughts, opinions and ideas. In a business world where people are paid to do a job and get stuff done, leaders will need to shift their focus and go to places outside of their comfort zone, to adapt their style, communicate in a way that resonates with others.

TIPS
- Businesses need to select leaders who have a genuine desire to be leaders and not on a reputation based on a technical skill or expertise
- Leaders will know how to be empathetic

Adding Value on the Journey

In the future, the value of leadership is not in the people processes, or what leaders do. The value of leadership will exist in the art of powerful dialogue, which can be defined as;

- Powerful dialogue is about supporting, challenging, stretching, adding perspective, and holding up a mirror.

- The ability to give clear and powerful feedback in a world of continuous learning.

- Listening is a hugely underutilised skill. Quietening the mind to really focus on what someone has to say, and then deciding how to respond in the moment will be a powerful skill.

- Coaching and the art of asking questions. Empowerment is to allow people to explore their own thought processes to get to their conclusion or solution.

To create a space for interaction that is genuine, authentic, honest, and powerful is one of the greatest leadership challenges, which occurs at the sweet spot of all the elements of leadership co-existing.

The impact of being a positive part of someone else's journey is the legacy that your leadership will leave. To be a leader that others seek to work with and want to be a part of the environment they create, to choose to invest their time and energy, to have developed on the journey is what will define great leadership in the future.

Leaders of the future will need courage - to do things differently, to take people on a journey and be a part of others' journeys. If it doesn't go to plan, a little humility is a good thing. Leaders will need to learn self-trust and self-forgiveness, in a world where we will relinquish control, focus on the outcome of where we're headed and enjoy the journey.

The world and technology are changing the future faster than we ever thought possible. This is disrupting and transforming our lives. The future of leadership is closer than you think.

TIPS

- Make it safe to communicate.
- Create new approaches to communication. Introduce new ways to communicate throughout your organization.
- Encourage and reward honest and open dialogue.

What Next?

Leaders with the 'human touch' will be a source of competitive advantage for your business in the future. Not only will they build value into their own personal brand, but they will add a much greater value through performance. Leadership capability directly impacts business performance.

A business pathway for Leadership Development –

Identifying the next step of your leadership journey

Use your business goals as start point

Complete a people SWOT analysis

Get Feedback - do an Employee Survey

Identify characteristics of great leadership for future success

Create a leadership vision

Build a leadership development programme - long term and bite size

Align the business to support the leadership vision

Provide support, learning resources

Keep learning

Role model - set the standard on what great leadership looks like

Gallup have estimated that the cost of a disengaged employee is 34% of their salary cost i.e. £3,400 for every £10,000 of an individuals' salary.

What is the next step for your business to develop its leadership capability?

Can you really afford not to?

Identifying next steps

Identify a goal for Leadership Development
What is the greatest Leadership Challenge?
What is the biggest gap you identify between current reality and future desired state?
What steps could you take to close the gap and move the business closer to the Leadership goal?
What is the one action you will take next?

To build a sustainable leadership culture requires a three phase approach:

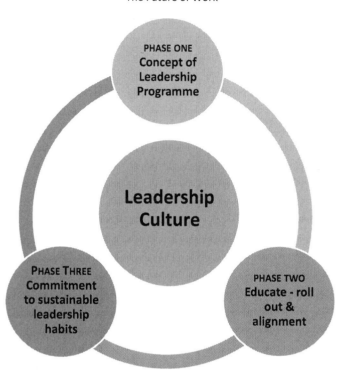

What is known is that leaders are required to juggle so many balls and often their leadership development falls into the 'important but not urgent' category. This is why consistently organisations fail to develop effective leadership capability. In the future, organisations will need to do things differently. To educate is not the same as embedding, commitment and action. Organisations who create the time and space for their leaders to do the learning, to educate, commit and take action in a sustainable way, over the long term in bite-size chunks are going to outperform their competitors.

TIPS

- Make leadership development a business priority as the future is closer than you think
- Develop a long term, bite-size programme that is focused on embedding the learning
- Create space for leaders to self-reflect throughout their leadership journey

About the author

Sian Perham BA(Hons) MCIPD

www.aligned-leadership.com

Sian Perham is a sought after Leadership specialist for Leaders in Business. She has helped hundreds of leaders realise their leadership potential. With over 20 years' experience working with leaders in organisations, Aligned Leadership understand being a leader requires the skills, behaviours and mindset to engage, inspire and motivate and excite others to high performance. Leaders who lead with a level of conscious thought, are aware of the impact they have on those around them, are able to flex their style, communicate with impact and be human – that is what makes great leadership.

Aligned Leadership works with individuals, teams and businesses to support and challenge individuals to be the best leaders they can be. Leaders who inspire, motivate and engage their teams. Leaders who understand that it's the people who are the competitive advantage in a business. Leaders who understand their value is in the quality dialogue they create for their teams; the performance dialogue, the powerful feedback, the development discussion, the coaching of their teams, the active listening. Improved working relationships, happier customers, work environments where people feel connection, trust and want to give their best performance.

Transforming the leadership pipeline

By Alasdair Graham

'Leaders don't create followers, they create more leaders'
Tom Peters

Jill Barad can do anything

Jill Barad was a marketing phenomenon for Mattel. She took over the Barbie line in 1982 when sales were flat and revitalised it with new packaging and accessories that encouraged girls to collect more and more dolls. In the mid-nineties she responded to criticism on Barbie being a poor role model for girls by creating new doctor, dentist and executive Barbies accompanied by the slogan 'We girls can do anything'. The Barbie line grew from $250 million in the eighties to $1.4 billion in 1995 when it accounted for 35% of Mattel's gross revenue. When Barad succeeded John Amerman as CEO in 1997 she was one of only four female CEOs in Fortune 500 companies. Her rise from arranging cosmetic store displays in the mid-seventies epitomised her own marketing slogan on female empowerment. So why did she resign just three years later?

While Barad's marketing skill was broadly recognised she was strongly criticised in other areas:

'When I've seen her at ad and marketing strategy meetings, everything she says improves the quality or the strategy. But as a long-term strategist and as a developer of people? No. An ability to accept an alternative point of view? No. Her demons presently are outweighing her assets, and I think the company is a lot the less for it.' Anonymous Mattel Executive, 1999

In September 1999 she led Mattel to acquire the Learning Company in a move into the high-tech toy market. It was expected to boost third quarter profits by up to $100 million, but instead there was a loss of $105 million. Mattel's market value dropped by $13.5 billion over the previous 18 months, and some shareholders filed lawsuits. The pressure from investors led the board to oust Barad in early 2000.

Barad's errors and problems as a CEO occurred because, despite her obvious marketing and product development talents, she had not sufficiently developed as a leader before taking on the role. She was perceived as a poor people manager and many Mattel executives resigned during her tenure. John Amerman, and Barad's previous managers in Mattel, should have developed her better for the CEO role. Mattel's leadership pipeline failed.

The case for a structured leadership pipeline

The case of Mattel and Barad is not unique. When M. Douglas Ivester was promoted to CEO at Coca-Cola in 1997 it seemed a natural move. He had been groomed by the previous CEO and served well as the CFO. He had a strong work ethic and detailed knowledge of the company. As with Barad he was forced to resign when key board members lost confidence in his leadership style. He was seen as inflexible and arrogant, and alienated the powerful bottlers who were needed to make Coca-Cola succeed. He loved big data before many knew its potential, but was unskilled at winning hearts and minds.

Leadership positions, particularly those at the head of an organisation, are very demanding. People management, strategy development, the essentials of finance and law, an understanding of the impact of technology, communicating and influencing skills are just some of the areas leaders are expected to master. It's not trivial to amass these capabilities, and in a 2011 American Management Association survey only 14% of respondents felt well prepared to deal with the loss of a senior manager.

To find people who meet these needs companies have broadly three options.

1. Recruit externally

This avoids the expense of leadership training and brings fresh ideas into the organisation, but will carry the cost of using head-hunters. People working inside the company will perceive this as a signal that they are not good enough to be promoted. Ambitious and talented individuals will leave to gain better external positions and the remaining talent pool will be significantly weaker.

2. Organic development

This involves simply promoting the best internal people for each leadership position as it becomes available. It sends a strong message that ambitious colleagues can stay inside the company to progress, but might not bring fresh ideas into the company. The key issue is that the people being promoted could be the best internal candidate, but as with Barad and Ivester they could have significant gaps in their capabilities.

3. Create a structured leadership pipeline

The final option involves a significant investment of money and time. A multi-step development programme is created which enables individuals with a high potential to gain the right combination of skills, experience and contacts to succeed at senior leadership roles. Each level of the pipeline is managed to ensure there are enough candidates for higher management roles, and the development tools and initiatives are proving effective.

Not surprisingly given the title of this book chapter, I recommend the third option. I recognise that this creates a major job for managers and HR departments, but would argue the essence of leadership is creating the next set of leaders. Option 1 is expensive, and the second option can prove disastrous as the case studies illustrate. A stronger leadership pipeline could have produced better candidates than Barad and Ivester for their companies, or involved a plan which enabled them to address development areas before they reached the executive suite. When creating a pipeline the company does not need to force individuals into jobs, but there will be a clear message that if someone wants to reach the top they will need certain competencies to be demonstrated in key roles.

Walter Mahler's path through the crossroads

The need for a leadership pipeline has been recognised in some companies for over forty years. Walter Mahler published *Executive Continuity* in the 1970s from working in General Electric on succession planning. His arguments influenced other organisations and were expanded by Ram Charan, Steve Drotter and Jim Noel.[15] The central idea was that leaders move through six crossroads on route to the top of an organisation:

---

[15] The Leadership Pipeline, Jossey-Bass, 2000

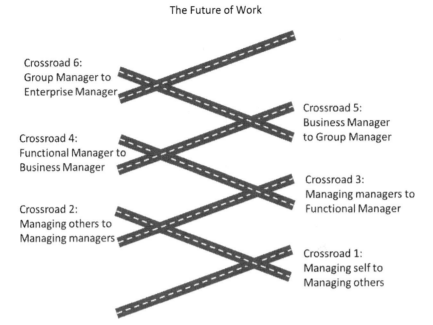

Crossroad 6:
Group Manager to
Enterprise Manager

Crossroad 5:
Business Manager
to Group Manager

Crossroad 4:
Functional Manager to
Business Manager

Crossroad 3:
Managing managers to
Functional Manager

Crossroad 2:
Managing others to
Managing managers

Crossroad 1:
Managing self to
Managing others

Figure 1 The Critical Career Crossroads from *The Leadership Pipeline* based on initial work from Walter Mahler

At each stage the manager is challenged to acquire new skills or approaches to succeed at that level of the organisation. Charan, Drotter and Noel articulate what they need to do, and the problems if they do not develop to meet the requirements of the role. When a clear model has been demonstrated in as reputable a company as GE it is troubling that today so many organisations still have problems with their leadership pipelines.

A fully functional pipeline will become even more important in the future because the demands on leaders will grow for four reasons:

1. Flexible work arrangements

More people will work part-time, or from home, or juggle multiple jobs. This will be driven both by the wishes of the employee to balance their life requirements, and the employer looking to meet business needs in a dynamic manner. A leader will need to inspire high individual performance levels and create a cohesive team from people who might see each other rarely. Team members managing a handful of jobs will not be able to commit everything to just one role, and this will challenge the traditional expectations of managers.

2. Diverse and dispersed teams

There is a laudable aim of increasing diversity in the workforce, and this will lead to more women in management, more workers with a Black, Asian or Minority Ethnicity (BAME), and greater levels of employment for people with physical and mental disabilities. Many larger European and American organisations seek to become more global in their management and work methods to be accepted in all of the markets for their products and services. This means an increase in the number of BAME managers, and a less westernised way of working. The leader of tomorrow will need to be aware of the varied cultures and backgrounds of their colleagues, and flex their management style appropriately while unifying their team around one vision. They will need to communicate effectively in person and at a distance, and using a mix of technologies including email, messages, and video.

3. Job displacement by technology

Robotics and AI will replace jobs previously thought to be too complex to automate. Natural areas under threat include rule-based sectors, such as accountancy and law, where knowledge of precedents or agreed practice are straight-forward to code. The increased sophistication of algorithms combined with highly efficient self-optimisation will extend job displacement to areas where human judgement is currently required. People will live with the uncertainty of whether their job, or even career, will be displaced. Managers will work with people going through the stress of saying goodbye to a job they have loved, and being forced to retrain. At times, a manager will wrestle with the difficult decision on whether to move from a human to a non-human method for a business activity. Managers will need to continually demonstrate the value of their skills since some traditional management activities, such as scheduling and budgeting, will be done more efficiently by an algorithm. Further into the future a leader could need to manage teams composed of human and non-human members.

4. Information overload

In 2013 it was estimated that 90% of all data in the world had been generated in the last two years[16]. By 2018 over 2.5 quintillion bytes of data were created every day[17]. At whatever date you read this sentence the data creation rate will be even higher, and will continue to grow rapidly. While big data will offer many benefits in the future, particularly with increasingly sophisticated AI to interrogate it, it will create some negative effects on people working. The constant flow of data packets to people will be intelligently optimised to produce reactions, and this will produce a dizzying stream of distractions that will hammer productivity. Team members will lurch from one notification to another and struggle to complete their tasks, and the manager's job of keeping everyone focused on meeting challenging goals will be much tougher. Leaders will have to manage their own

---

[16] SINTEF. "Big Data, for better or worse: 90% of world's data generated over last two years." ScienceDaily. ScienceDaily, 22 May 2013.
[17] Domo, "Data never sleeps" 6th Edition, 2017

information deluge and pick out the key pieces of data from the mass of distraction.

The pipeline of the future

To create the leaders of the future, and withstand the challenges described, the pipeline of the future needs to be:

A. Flexible. A small organisation will not have the six levels presented in the career crossroads, and instead could have important transitions which happen at the same level of hierarchy. Unlike the height of GE's success, few people will stay with one company their whole career so the pipeline should accommodate workers who might join or re-join the company after gaining valuable experience elsewhere. Technology companies could see the benefit of having separate pipelines for technical and people management, and a controlled method for moving between them.

B. Dynamic. As businesses grow, merge, divest or change their models the pipeline should adapt to provide the right leaders to meet the new demands. A new technology could replace or transform a part of the company, and talented potential leaders will need to make difficult transitions. The launch of a new product to disrupt a traditional industry could call on new mind- or skillsets to make the most of the opportunity. In all cases the pipeline needs to update quickly.

C. Inclusive. The lack of women in senior management roles, and the sluggish rate of improvement in this, shows that too many pipelines have been filled primarily with the same demographic as the existing leaders. While this might involve unconscious bias instead of conscious discrimination, the damage to organisations remains the same: the best people do not always become leaders. Leadership pipelines should have inclusivity metrics and progressive goals towards a reasonable representation based on the industry and countries in which the company works.

D. Managed by data. A well-stocked pipeline is a business asset, and a poorly stocked one is a liability. Each level of hierarchy, or leadership capability, should have a target for the number of people who could reach the next level. Senior leaders and HR have a collective responsibility for restocking an empty level, or removing a clogged level which could encourage ambitious people below it to leave. Development programmes should demonstrate their cost effectiveness over recruiting externally via head-hunters.

The leadership landscape

While a pipeline might have been a suitable metaphor for the structured and standardised development of many leaders in the past, it does not represent the flexible, dynamic and person-centred manner leaders should grow in the future:

- Senior leaders will gain the experience and skills in different orders instead of a standard and linear sequence
- People need to agree on their development instead of being pushed through the pipeline
- Leaders can enter and leave the development process at different points particularly as they leave and join the organisation

131

A more apt metaphor is a leadership landscape. Travelling through the parts of the landscape will deliver the key experiences that a senior leader needs, and the landscape will vary by the organisation structure and sector. The example leadership landscape presented in *Figure 2* shows a company in which a senior leader needs to have delivered tangible business benefits in line management, group management, operations, account management, and strategy development. Some parts of the landscape should be travelled to in a sequence (e.g. line management before group management), but there will be flexibility in the order of visiting areas.

Figure 2 Example of a leadership landscape

The leadership landscape should create a vivid, unique and memorable map for ambitious people in the company to embrace.

Key tools to use

The list below is not intended to be an exhaustive examination of all possible development methods, but will instead highlight a small number of approaches which can have a strong impact in helping people move about the leadership landscape.

1. Strength-based personal development

As people travel through the landscape and face new challenges they will be addressing development areas, but an exclusive focus on what they find most difficult can be demotivating. Instead, individuals should explore their personal strengths early in their careers and seek to apply these in new roles. This will allow them to understand their unique leadership presence and how they help the organisation and their colleagues. The strength diagnostic used should have sections relevant to both the individual, and the values important to the organisation.

2. Integrated training programmes

Class-based training programmes will continue to play an important role in leadership development since they can provide an engaging and focused learning experience. However, sometimes these are standalone events with little connection to the leader's current goals. They can also represent a significant investment in time and money so should deliver a clear benefit. To make these fit-for-purpose for the future they should be closely integrated into the attendees' current job:

- Prepare for each training programme with the leader or HR partner to agree pre-course goals
- Support the participant as they turn the lessons into actions
- Evaluate the success rate of the goals and which further development will be beneficial

The full sequence can be represented as:

Preparation → Course → Implementation with Support → Evaluation

People should attend virtual sessions whenever face-to-face interaction is not critical particularly due to the increasingly immersive nature of virtual and augmented environments.

The implementation should include a test of the individual's ability to meet the challenges of the next role or level of leadership. Support, including mentoring and coaching, should improve the ability of the leader to successfully meet the challenges.

3. Mentoring

A mentor will help someone in their career understand the overall leadership landscape and the career plan which is right for them. The mentor will guide people as they journey through the landscape picking up vital skills and experiences. It's possible that one part of the landscape will appeal to the leader far more than others, and they might want to settle there.

In the past mentors have been very experienced people inside a company. In the future this should include:

- Retirees with an informed and objective perspective of the company
- Respected external mentors who have a good industry knowledge
- Individuals with similar life paths to those desired by the mentees

Mentors will change as the career goals, and life situation, grows and changes.

4. Coaching

Coaching is one of the fastest growing and most effective development tools. The ability to have remote and/or virtual coaching sessions improves its cost effectiveness, and it can be applied in many situations. As a leader moves through the landscape coaching should accompany every significant change to allow leaders to face the behavioural changes required. Coaching helps people face the emotional intensity of leadership, and explore fresh perspectives to face the new challenges. Unlike mentoring, coaching should not be a continual support. It should be used to make the specific skill jumps and understand and succeed in the new environments around the landscape.

5. Leadership community

The internal leadership community is a source of advice and assistance to people as they develop in different parts of the map. As individuals become more senior their network, and the knowledge and resources it offers, becomes more potent than their own knowledge. This should be nurtured to allow greater collaboration and social learning to flourish.

The development tools described should be carefully assessed to ensure the overall landscape is cost effective for the organisation. Each part of the landscape can be owned by a senior leader or HR professional who continually improves it, and decides how the tools available can be utilised.

In summary

The leadership pipeline is a powerful concept which was well used in GE, and successfully influenced many companies. To meet the work needs of the future it should transform into a tailored, dynamic and vibrant landscape through which leaders travel. This will turn the stories of executives who were not developed to meet the highest demands, into tales of successful leaders helping their people and companies to thrive.

About the author

Dr Alasdair Graham

www.apexdiscovery.com

Alasdair has over twenty years of leadership and management experience from the petrochemicals and media industries. His initial training was in science, and he then broadened his skills in commercial roles including buying a billion dollars of refinery products and the selling of performance additives for automotive lubricants. Alasdair now runs Apex Discovery which offers consultancy, coaching and training for leaders seeking to make a difference with their teams or companies. Alasdair also helps people rediscover lost energy, or build a career plan in which they believe. He can be contacted through his website or on LinkedIn.

When not working Alasdair enjoys Latin dancing, hillwalking and bagging Munros with his family, and following Heart of Midlothian. The latter offers more pain than pleasure.

41995632R00082

Printed in Poland
by Amazon Fulfillment
Poland Sp. z o.o., Wrocław